Moonchildren

A COMIC PLAY IN TWO ACTS

By Michael Weller

SAMUEL FRENCH, INC.

45 WEST 25TH STREET   NEW YORK 10010

7623 SUNSET BOULEVARD   HOLLYWOOD 90046

LONDON   *TORONTO*

Originally published in Great Britain under the title CANCER by Faber & Faber Ltd.

Copyright © 1971 by Michael Weller

ALL RIGHTS RESERVED

ISBN 0 573 61245-5   Printed in U.S.A.

MOONCHILDREN was first presented on **February 21, 1972** at the Royale Theatre by David Merrick. The director was Alan Schneider, with settings by William Ritman and lighting by Martin Aronstein. The original cast was as follows:

THE CAST
(*In Order of Speaking*)

THE STUDENTS

MIKE	*Kevin Conway*
RUTH	*Maureen Anderman*
COOTIE (MEL)	*Edward Herrmann*
NORMAN	*Christopher Guest*
DICK	*Stephen Collins*
KATHY	*Jill Eikenberry*
BOB RETTIE (JOB)	*James Woods*
SHELLY	*Cara Duff-MacCormick*

THE OTHERS

RALPH	*Donegan Smith*
MR. WILLIS	*Robert Prosky*
LUCKY	*Ronald McLarty*
BREAM	*Louis Zorich*
EFFING	*Peter Alzado*
UNCLE MURRY	*Salem Ludwig*
COOTIE'S FATHER	*George Curley*
MILKMAN	*Michael Tucker*

The place is a student apartment in an American university town.

The time is around 1965-66.

3

THE CAST

MAIN PEOPLE

BOB RETTIE (JOB)
MIKE
COOTIE (MEL)
RUTH
KATHY
DICK
NORMAN
SHELLY

THE OTHERS

RALPH, *a young salesman who lives at home*
MR. WILLIS, *the landlord*
LUCKY, *the guy who lives downstairs*
EFFING, *a rookie cop*
BREAM, *an old-timer cop*
UNCLE MURRY, *Bob's uncle*
COOTIE'S FATHER
MILKMAN

ACT ONE

SCENE 1: Early evening. Fall.
SCENE 2: A few weeks later. Morning.
SCENE 3: That afternoon.
SCENE 4: Early evening. Before Christmas.

ACT TWO

SCENE 1: An afternoon after Christmas.
SCENE 2: Before graduation.
SCENE 3: An afternoon after graduation.

4

Moonchildren

ACT ONE

Scene 1

The stage is dark. You can't see anything.

MIKE. (*Whisper.*) I heard something. She definitely made a noise.

RUTH. (*Whisper.*) Shut up.

MIKE. (*Whisper.*) I'm telling you, I know the noise they make. That was it.

COOTIE. I read somewhere about how they can see in the dark.

RUTH. (*Whisper.*) I never read that.

COOTIE. No shit . . .

RUTH. . . . Shhh . . .

COOTIE. (*Whisper.*) . . . I read how they got these hundreds of thousands of millions of tiny, submicroscopic, photosensitive cells in each eyeball, so when it gets dark they can just turn on these cells and see like it was daytime.

MIKE. (*Whisper.*) He's right, Ruth. Hey, Cootie, you're right. I remember reading that in a back issue of the *Vertebrate Review*.

COOTIE. (*Whisper.*) That's it. That's the one. Special eyeball issue.

MIKE. (*Whisper.*) Yeah, yeah, July.

RUTH. (*Whisper.*) You guys must be pretty stupid if you really believe that. What do you think they have whiskers for? The whole point of whiskers in the first place is so you can get around in the dark. That's why

5

they stick out so far, so you don't go bumping into things, chairs and refrigerators and that.

MIKE. (*Whisper.*) Hey, shh. I think she's starting.

RUTH. Don't tell me "shhh."

MIKE. O.K. I'm sorry.

RUTH. So shut up if she's starting.

(*A pause.*)

COOTIE. (*Whisper.*) I was just thinking, how are we gonna see her when she starts giving birth?

RUTH. (*Whisper.*) Jesus, how stupid can you get! We'll turn on the light.

COOTIE. Yeah, but the whole thing is, how do we know when to turn on the light? Like, what if we're too early?

MIKE. (*Whisper.*) Or too late.

COOTIE. (*Whisper.*) Yeah, what if we're too late?

MIKE. (*Whisper.*) Or right in the middle . . .

COOTIE. (*Whisper.*) Holy shit, yeah, what if we flip on the old lights when she's halfway through a severe uterine contraction. She'll go apeshit and clamp up and kill the kitten.

RUTH. (*Whisper.*) Hey, shut up, you guys, willya? Willya shut up?

MIKE. There's probably a more scientific way to watch a cat give birth.

RUTH. (*Loud whisper.*) Everybody shut the fuck up.

(*A long pause.*)

NORMAN. How much longer are you guys gonna have the lights out?

COOTIE. Jesus Christ, Norman, why do you have to go skulking around like that?

NORMAN. I'm not skulking. I'm just sitting here. Maybe you didn't notice when you came in, but I was reading this book. I mean, I thought you were only gonna have the lights out for maybe a few minutes or something, but that was over an hour ago . . . and I really can't read very well with the lights off. I mean . . . you know . . .

COTTIE. Norman, you try to rush a cat when it's giving birth and you come smack up against nature. (*Makes a popping or slapping noise like something coming smack up against nature.*)

MIKE. Norman . . .

NORMAN. What?

MIKE. Don't fight nature, Norman.

NORMAN. I'm not. I'm just trying to read this book.

(A pause.)

COOTIE. Is it a good book?

RUTH. (*Loud whisper.*) For chrissakes, what's the matter with everyone?

NORMAN. (*Whisper.*) It's pretty good. I don't follow all of it. It's written in a funny kind of way so you forget a lot of it right after you've read it. The guys up in the Mathematics Department say it's supposed to be pretty good. I don't know, though.

COOTIE. The thing is, Norman, you see the entire miracle of birth in cats, taken from initial labor to the biting off of the umbilical cord and the lapping up of the afterbirth can often take an entire night.

RUTH. (*Loud whisper.*) Brother, you try to get a few guys to shut up for a little while . . .

MIKE. (*Yelling.*) Hey, c'mon, everyone, cut the shit, let's have a little quiet around here. I don't want to see anyone panic and start running in all different directions trampling on innocent women and children . . .

RUTH. I swear to Christ, Mike, if you don't shut up I'll kill you.

MIKE. O.K.

(*The hall door is opened from outside and a shaft of light falls across the middle of the room, dimly high-lighting MIKE, COOTIE and RUTH crouched around a cardboard carton on the floor, and NORMAN sitting at the kitchen table. The moment* DICK *opens the door,* NORMAN *bends his book toward the light to cop a few sentences.*)

RUTH. Hey, c'mon, shut the door, Dick.
COOTIE. Shut the fucking door.
MIKE. (*Brief pause.*) We'd really like you to shut the door, Richard.

(DICK *enters and shuts the door. Silence. Seconds later the stage is lit again, this time from an icebox that* DICK *opened, which has an automatic light inside.* DICK *squats before the icebox while the others watch. The kitchen can be dimly seen now. The icebox is ancient, dating from the days when electricity was replacing the iceman; a box on legs with a barrel-shape cooler on top. On the door, perhaps not yet visible, is written GOD IS COOL. Hundreds of empty two quart milk bottles line the walls, layer upon layer with planks in between each level. It's a deliberate construction. The floor is imitation cork vinyl tiles, alternating light and dark like a chess board, but the floor is only half finished. Where the tiles end irregularly, as if work was stopped suddenly, there is a border of black tile glue, by now hard, then rough plank flooring. The kitchen table is round, and set about with six unmatched chairs. Clutter. Posters. A map of Europe on one wall. Telephone hung on the wall. Sink full of dirty dishes. A pad and pencil hang by the icebox. Everyone uses the kitchen in a particular way. So* DICK *is squatting before the open icebox.*)

RUTH. That's very cute, Richard.
MIKE. C'mon, shut the icebox. We were in here first.
NORMAN. I was reading when you guys came in.

(DICK *looks over his shoulder at them briefly, then back into the icebox.*)

COOTIE. Dick, in my humble opinion you're a miserable shit and a party pooper.

DICK. (*Standing.*) All right, now listen. I went down to the Star Supermarket this afternoon and I got a four-dozen pack of frozen hamburgers. That's forty-eight. When I looked just now there were only forty-three and I only had two of them for dinner tonight.

RUTH. And you never washed up.

MIKE. (*Intensely interested.*) Hey, Dick, are those Star Hamburgers any good?

DICK. And by the way, I've been keeping count since the beginning of the semester. It's getting near fifty hamburgers I can't account for.

COOTIE. Jesus, Dick, you should've said something before this.

DICK. Look, I'm not about to make a stink about a couple of hamburgers here and there, but Jesus Christ, almost sixty of them. I'm putting it down on common stock and we're all gonna pay for it. (*Turns on the light.*)

RUTH. Dick, willya turn out the light, please?

DICK. I'm sorry, I've lost too many hamburgers. I'm putting down for four dozen. (*Goes to the pad by the icebox and starts writing.*)

RUTH. Now will you turn out the light?

DICK. (*Turns in disgust.*) Who put peanut butter down on common stock?

MIKE. I did. I got a jar of chunky last Thursday and when I opened it on Saturday someone had already been in there.

DICK. Well, I never had any of your peanut butter. I'm not paying for it.

MIKE. Well, I never had any of your goddamn eight hundred hamburgers either. . . .

COOTIE. I seem to remember having some chunky peanut butter on Friday. Was your peanut butter brown . . .

MIKE. Yeah, light brown with little chunks of . . .

(KATHY *enters through the front door with a green book
    bag slung over her shoulder.*)

KATHY. Oh boy, look out for Bob. (*Crosses the room
heading for the hall door.*)

RUTH. What's wrong with Bob?

KATHY. He's in a really shitty mood. I've seen him act
weird before but this is, I don't know, it's pretty bad.

MIKE. Where is he?

COOTIE. Yeah, where's Bob?

MIKE. Good old Bob.

COOTIE. Where's good old Bob?

KATHY. And fuck you too, I'm serious.

NORMAN. Boy, I really can't absorb very much with
everyone talking.

KATHY. We were just sitting there, you know, in Hum
105 and that ass-hole Meyerson starts in with the crap
about the cosmic equation . . .

NORMAN. What's the cosmic equation?

RUTH. (*Ignoring* NORMAN.) Why'd that upset Bob?

KATHY. I don't know. That's the thing . . . it's weird.

DICK. I bet Bob's responsible for some of my hamburgers. I notice you and him never go shopping for
dinner.

KATHY. He just seems to be kind of . . . it's really
weird. Like today, you know . . . well, I mean, hasn't
anyone noticed anything?

MIKE. You're right, Kathy. He's stopped using my
toothpaste.

COOTIE. Started using mine.

KATHY. Look, I'm not kidding around. He could be
cracking up or something.

(BOB *enters through the front door carrying his books.
    He looks fine. Everyone stares at him.*)

MIKE. Hi, Bob.

RUTH. Hi, Bob.

COOTIE. Hi, Bob.

NORMAN. Hello, Bob.

BOB. (*Pause.*) Hi, Mike, hi, Ruth, hi, Cootie, hello, Norman. Hi, Dick.

DICK. Listen, do you know anything about . . .

BOB. No, I haven't touched your fucking hamburgers.

MIKE. How you been, good old Bob?

COOTIE. How's the old liver and the old pancreas and the old pituitary, and the . . . ?

BOB. Is there any mail?

COOTIE. There's this really big package from Beirut. It took four guys to get it up the stairs.

MIKE. We think it's a harp.

RUTH. There's a letter in your room. (BOB *looks at them quizzically, then goes out down the hall.* KATHY *shoots them a glance, then follows.*) Hey, I think Kathy's right. There's definitely something wrong with Bob.

MIKE. So what?

COOTIE. Yeah, fuck Bob.

MIKE. Fuck good old Bob.

NORMAN. Maybe he's worried about the future. (*They look at* NORMAN.) I mean, you know, maybe he's worried about it. I don't know him all that well. Just, you know, maybe he's worried about what he's gonna do when, you know, after he graduates and everything.

DICK. He ought to be worried.

MIKE. You bet your ass he ought to be. Same goes for all you guys, even you, Dick. And, Cootie, you ought to be worried. I ought to be worried. I am. I'm fucking petrified. You watch what happens at the graduation ceremonies. There's gonna be this line of green military busses two miles long parked on the road outside and they're gonna pick us up and take us to Vietnam and we'll be walking around one day in the depths of the rain forest looking out for wily enemy snipers and carnivorous insects and tropical snakes that can eat a whole moose in one gulp and earthworms sixteen feet long and one day when we least expect it this wily old sniper'll leap out from behind a blade of grass and . . . powie! right in the head. (*Pause.*) I'm worried.

DICK. Anyone that can spell can get out of Vietnam.

NORMAN. They can't get me. I'm in graduate school.

DICK. Norman, you couldn't buy your way into the army.

NORMAN. I wouldn't go.

MIKE. Why wouldn't you go, Norman?

NORMAN. Huh?

COOTIE. Yeah, think of the army. What about them? They need good mathematics graduate students out there in the marshes of Quac Thop Chew Hoy Ben Van Pho Quay Gup Trin.

NORMAN. I don't agree with the war.

MIKE. Oh, for god's sake, then let's stop it.

NORMAN. I had my physical and everything. I passed. I could've pretended I was insane or something.

DICK. Pretended?

RUTH. Hey, doesn't anyone around here give a shit about Bob?

MIKE. O.K. Everyone that gives a shit, raise your hand. (COOTIE, MIKE *and* DICK, *then* NORMAN, *raise their hands.*) See, we all give a shit. So what should we do?

RUTH. Well, I don't know. Maybe we ought to try and find out what's troubling him.

DICK. Maybe he doesn't want us to know. Just maybe.

COOTIE. Yeah, what if he's teetering on the brink of a complete schizophrenic withdrawal and the only thing keeping him sane is knowing that we don't know what's troubling him?

MIKE. It's our duty as classmates and favorite turds to leave him alone.

RUTH. Maybe something's wrong between him and Kathy.

DICK. Like what?

RUTH. I don't know. That's what I'm asking.

DICK. He doesn't give a shit about her. Not really. She's just a good lay, that's all.

RUTH. How would you know, Dick?

NORMAN. I thought they were in love.

DICK. Jesus, Norman, where the hell is your head at?

NORMAN. Huh?

MIKE. "Define the problem, then solve it."

COOTIE. Yeah, right. What's troubling good old Bob?

MIKE. I think we all oughta go to bed tonight with notebooks under our pillows and when we get a well-focused and comprehensive idea about the central dilemma of Bob's existence we ought to write it down in clear, concise sentences with particular attention to grammar and punctuation.

COOTIE. Then we can meet in here tomorrow and pool our insights.

MIKE. That's a really great plan. Hey, gang, how about it?

RUTH. All I want to know is what's the trouble?

DICK. All I want to know is who the fuck's eating my hamburgers?

NORMAN. Why don't you talk to him?

RUTH. What?

NORMAN. I mean, you know, Bob. If you want to find out what's troubling him probably the best thing to do is talk to him and ask him, well, "What's troubling you" or something like that and if he feels like talking about it he can and if he doesn't . . . well . . .

RUTH. (Vague.) Yeah, maybe I'll do that.

NORMAN. That's what I'd do if I wanted to know. I mean, I'm not saying I wouldn't like to know what's troubling him. I mean, if you find out I'd be very interested to . . . (MIKE is at the cat box.)

MIKE. Jesus Christ. Jesus H. Fucking Christ.

NORMAN. What's wrong?

MIKE. She wasn't even in there. (Flips the top open quickly.)

COOTIE. You mean all that time we were looking at an empty box in the dark and she wasn't even in there?

MIKE. She must've snuck out while we had our backs turned.

COOTIE. Sneaky little beastie.

MIKE. Cootie, you don't understand. She might be out there in the road *right now*.

COOTIE. Right now.

MIKE. With all the traffic . . .

(COOTIE *and* RUTH *both get the signal at once and start for the hall door to get ready to go out.*)

COOTIE. . . . and the architects driving home drunk from seeing their mistresses . . .

MIKE. Scanning the road for pregnant cats to run over.

(MIKE *and* COOTIE *exit down the hall.* RUTH *takes her coat off a chair and starts to put it on.* DICK *watches her.*)

DICK. Hey, you haven't done the essay for Phil 540. (*Pause.*) It's due tomorrow.

RUTH. So what?

NORMAN. Is that a good course, Philosophy 540?

RUTH. Nope. Professor Quinn is an albino dwarf queer with halitosis and he smokes too much.

DICK. He does not.

RUTH. Three packs of Pall Mall a day is too much. He's gonna die of cancer.

DICK. He's a genius.

RUTH. You have a thing about queers.

DICK. Fuck off, Ruth.

RUTH. You started it.

(MIKE *and* COOTIE *storm in dressed in some outrageous version of cat-hunting gear.* RUTH *joins them.*)

COOTIE. Boy, if we're too late I hate to think of all the dead cats we'll have on our conscience.

MIKE. You gonna help, Dick?

DICK. Fuck off.

MIKE. How 'bout you, Norman, aren't you gonna do your bit for the world of cats?

NORMAN. I'm just in the middle of this chapter. (MIKE *and* COOTIE *shake their heads in disapproval and go out with* RUTH. DICK *has a banana which he peels slowly while watching* NORMAN *read.* NORMAN *sees him out of the side of his eye and tries to ignore him.* DICK *chews loudly.*) Hey, it's pretty hard to concentrate when someone's watching you, you know.

DICK. How come you're reading that book?

NORMAN. I don't know. It's supposed to be pretty good.

DICK. What are you gonna do when you finish it?

NORMAN. (*Thinks.*) I'll start another.

DICK. Yeah, but what happens when you forget this one? It'll be as if you hadn't ever read it, so what's the point?

NORMAN. Oh, I don't know. I happen to believe you learn things even when you don't know it. Like, if you read something, well, I am reading something right now and maybe I'll forget some of it. . . . I mean there's a lot of it I can't remember already but I'm still being altered in lots of little ways I may not even be aware of because of, well, you know, books, experiences . . . (*Pause.*) Life.

DICK. Don't you ever get the feeling you're completely irrelevant?

NORMAN. No. I don't think so.

DICK. I mean you go into the mathematics department every day and sit there looking out the window and thinking about cars and women and every now and then a couple of numbers pop into your head but whenever you come up with a good problem to work on you find out there's all these Chinese guys running up and down the hallways, solving all the problems worth solving while you sit there wondering what the hell you're doing. (*That's all in one rush.* NORMAN *is dumbstruck.*)

NORMAN. No, it's not like that. (*Pause.*) Well, you know, it's just not that simple. (*Pause.*) How do you know all that?

DICK. Oh, you know. . . .

NORMAN. Are you doing anything relevant?

DICK. You can't get more relevant than Far Eastern Studies. That's where everything's happening. Ask me anything about the far east and I'll tell you the answer. China, Vietnam, Cambodia, Japan, Korea, you name it.

NORMAN. I guess I ought to know more about those things. I don't know, I keep thinking there's a lot of things I should know about.

DICK. The thing is, Norman, the way I see it, you're already deeply committed to the system. You take away black ghettos, stop the war in Vietnam, distribute the wealth equally throughout the country and *you* wouldn't be in graduate school.

NORMAN. (*Curious.*) I wouldn't?

DICK. You don't know anything about what makes it all work, do you? (*Chucks the banana peel in the cat box and starts out.*)

NORMAN. Hey, you shouldn't throw that in there.

DICK. Why not?

NORMAN. Well, I mean, that's the box for the cat. Maybe she won't want to have her kittens on a banana peel.

DICK. Norman, how long have you been living here?

NORMAN. Three months. No, a little longer, three months and two weeks altogether.

DICK. Have you ever seen a cat around here?

NORMAN. Well, I don't know. I'm out a lot of the time.

DICK. Norman, there is no cat. We don't have a cat. Boy, for a graduate student you got a lot to learn. Jesus. (*Walks out down the hall.*)

(NORMAN, *confused, goes to the cat box and looks into
it. He then looks up and around the room. LIGHTS
DIM.*)

END OF SCENE ONE

ACT ONE

SCENE 2

A few days later.

NORMAN *is reading.* RUTH *is making sandwiches.* COOTIE
and MIKE *are fussing over a banner.*

COOTIE. I don't know about the wording.

MIKE. You're unhappy about the wording.

COOTIE. Well, I'm not, you know, cut up about it or
anything, but I'm definitely not as happy as I could be.

RUTH. Who wants orange marmalade?

MIKE. I'd like an orange marmalade.

COOTIE. I want two orange marmalade and two chunky
peanut butter please.

RUTH. How 'bout you, Norman?

COOTIE. And I wouldn't mind a chunky peanut butter
and orange marmalade mixed.

RUTH. Hey, Norman, do you want sandwiches or not?

COOTIE. If you're coming you gotta have sandwiches
handy. On your average march you find you get through
a good two peanut butter and jellies before you even get
to where you're supposed to demonstrate, and then after
circling around and yelling militant slogans at the monu-
ment or park or poison gas plant or nuclear establishment
for a couple of hours, you find you're just about ready
for another peanut butter and jelly . . .

MIKE. Or cream cheese and olives.

COOTIE. Or bacon, lettuce and tomato.

MIKE. On toast.

COOTIE. Hold the mayonnaise. I mean, I know you meet a lot of moderate to extremely groovy people at a march, but you can never count on them having extra sandwiches for a new acquaintance.

RUTH. Hey, Norman, would you just tell me if you're coming with us or not?

NORMAN. (*Unfriendly.*) I'm going with Dick.

COOTIE. (*Pause.*) You're lucky there. You'll get hamburger on toasted roll if you go with Dick. He takes Sterno and cooks right out there in the middle of lines of charging cops and tear gas and mace and everything.

(DICK *enters.*)

MIKE. Hey, Dick, you better hurry up and get dressed for the march.

COOTIE. Yeah, you don't want to be late or all the best ass'll be grabbed up.

(DICK *goes to the banner.* MIKE *blocks his view of it.*)

DICK. What's it say?

MIKE. "But government bonds."

RUTH. You want some of our peanut butter and marmalade?

MIKE. What's this about giving away all our peanut butter and marmalade all of a sudden? He wouldn't give us any of his lousy hamburgers. We had to pay for 'em outta common stock.

DICK. Where's Kathy and Bob?

MIKE. Yeah, where's good old Bob? (*Goes to the hall door and yells down.*) Hey, you guys, are you coming?

KATHY. (*Off.*) Yeah, hold on a minute, willya?

MIKE. They're coming.

COOTIE. Norman, I've been watching you pretty closely for the last few days and I have this definite impression you've been displaying hostility towards me, Mike and Ruth, in that order.

NORMAN. I'm just reading this boo(k) . . .

COOTIE. Don't be negative, Norman. You're trying to pretend I hadn't noticed your emotions, but you happen to be up against a disciple of Freud, Jung, Adler, Pavlov, Skinner and the honorable L. Ron Hubbard, to mention but a few. It just so happens I can detect subatomic trace particles of hostility within a siv-mile radius of anywhere I am.

MIKE. It's no use contradicting him, Norman. If he says he can feel hostility, that's it. I mean, even I can feel hostility, and I'm not particularly sensitive in that direction.

NORMAN. I'm not feeling hostile. . . .

COOTIE. You're not only feeling it. You're dying to tell us about it. That's a basic axiom of hostility.

NORMAN. Oh, brother, you guys.

DICK. Leave him alone.

COOTIE. Dick, that is the worst thing you can do. I know you think you're being a good shit and everything, but if the guy is riddled with hostility and he doesn't get it out of his system it's gonna go haywire and zing all around inside his body 'til he's 28 years old and then he'll get cancer.

RUTH. We're really gonna be late if those guys don't hurry up.

MIKE. That reminds me of a guy I was reading about. He got so pent up with hostility his head fell right down into his body, no shit, that's what I was reading, right down between his shoulders.

COOTIE. Fell?

MIKE. Yeah, straight down, 'til all you could see were these two little eyeballs peering out over his collarbone.

COOTIE. Mike.

MIKE. What, Mel?

COOTIE. Fell?

MIKE. Sank?

COOTIE. Subsided.

MIKE. Yeah, right. . . .

COOTIE. In fact, as I remember it his head eventually disappeared completely.

MIKE. Don't rush me. I'm coming to that. Now, Norman, you should pay particularly close attention because this case tells us something very important about life in these feverish times. See, everybody used to tell this guy, loosen up, see an analyst, but the guy refused. Why? Cost too much. And that turned out to be really crooked economic thinking because with his head inside him like that he couldn't see where he was going and he had to hire a guy full time, seven days a week, just to lead him 'round.

COOTIE. There was a very fine article about that guy in the *Hostility Journal,* spring number. Did you happen to catch that article, Norman?

NORMAN. I'm not listening.

MIKE. Did it tell what happened to him?

COOTIE. Well, you know, it was one of those articles in two parts, and wouldn't you know it, that's just when my subscription ran out.

MIKE. Oh, well, you missed the best part. See, when his head got down as far . . . subsided . . . as far as his stomach . . .

COOTIE. Thank you.

MIKE. . . . he went and hired a top-notch transplant surgeon to replace his belly button with a flexible, clear plastic window so he could see where he was going.

COOTIE. Jumpin' Jehoshaphat ! ! ! !

MIKE. And I'm happy to announce the operation was a complete success.

COOTIE. Leapin' lizards.

MIKE. In a matter of weeks the wound healed, no signs of tissue rejection with the plastic window and he was able to lead a completely normal life again, skin diving, stamp collecting . . . a lot of political work.

COOTIE. Ods bodikins, I'll be bound . . .

MIKE. He could even go to the movies when he felt like it except that he had to sit up on the back of the seat, which caused a lot of hard feeling among the people sitting directly behind him.

COOTIE. Gosh-a-rootie.

MIKE. But that is the wonderful thing about the modern movie going public; they respected his infirmity.

COOTIE. Fuck a duck.

MIKE. Shut up, sonny boy, I ain't finished yet.

COOTIE. There's more?

MIKE. Yeah. You see, the really incredible thing was when this guy woke up one morning and realized his head was still sinking . . .

COOTIE. . . . subsiding . . .

MIKE. . . . and he went to see his doctor to have it checked out.

RUTH. Mike, come on . . .

MIKE. He was just walking along the street, you know, and he came to this corner and stopped for a red light and this dog came along and peed on his leg. The man bent forward to see what was making his pants wet and just then a workman up on some scaffolding directly behind him dropped a pipe wrench on his back, and the impact of this wrench, plus the deeply inclined position of the guy's upper body, knocked his head right back into place.

COOTIE. Hot diggity! !

MIKE. Well, the guy went apeshit, jumping all over the place, singing and dancing away right out there in the street . . . and that's just when it all had to happen . . .

RUTH. Mike!

MIKE. This poor guy, after all his suffering was finally looking forward to a normal and happy life . . .

COOTIE. Oh, shit, yeah, I remember . . .

MIKE. Yeah, you 'member, he was just standing out there in the street, stopping traffic from both directions, tears of humble gratitude streaming down his cheeks when all of a sudden, right out of the blue some dumb bastard comes . . . (BOB *and* KATHY *have entered from the hallway, ready for the march.* MIKE *sees them, stops his story and casually greets them on his way to putting on his coat.*) Hi, Bob, hi, Kathy, you guys ready?

RUTH. Hey, do you want some of our peanut butter and marmalade?

BOB. I have an announcement.

COOTIE. Well, we used to have a near-sighted canary that kept flying into . . .

RUTH. Listen, I gotta make these sandwiches and we're gonna end up short if I don't got some co-operation around here.

COOTIE. Hey, look, Norman doesn't have a banner. Norman, aren't you gonna bring a banner?

BOB. Mel, will you please shut up? I want to say something.

COOTIE. Well, fuck you, I'm talking to Norman. You want him to get all the way down to the demonstration and they disqualify him because he doesn't have a banner?

RUTH. All right, everyone is gonna fucking well eat whatever I make.

MIKE. (*Yelling.*) All right, all right, everybody stay where you are, don't move, let's have a little order around here. (*Pause.*) Okay, Bob, I think we got everything under control now.

BOB. Thank you.

MIKE. That's okay, Bob.

BOB. Look, I just wanted to . . .

MIKE. Bob?

BOB. What?

MIKE. Anytime.

BOB. Thank you, Mike.

MIKE. That's okay, Bob, you're a good shit.

BOB. (*Halting.*) Look, I was just wondering . . . well, I . . .

MIKE. Do you want water or anything?

RUTH. For chrissakes, Mike, shut up.

COOTIE. (*Cooling things.*) Yeah, shut your mouth, sonny boy, yer creatin' a public nuisance.

RUTH. Go on, Bob.

BOB. No, no, look, it's no big deal. I just . . . Norman, if there is one way to remain irrelevant and ineffective, it's to sit with your nose buried in a book while life is raging all around you. (NORMAN *looks up and closes his book, bewildered.*) Thank you. Okay. Announcement. (*Tries to find a way to say what he has to say. He paces for a moment, frames the thought and begins to speak. Before a sound is out, though . . .*)

MIKE. "Earthquakes in Singapore."

RUTH. (*With incredible rage.*) SHUT UP!

BOB. Never mind.

MIKE. Sorry. I'm sorry.

RUTH. What is it, Bob?

BOB. Nothing. Really, nothing at all. Just a kind of funny thing I was thinking the other day during a Humanities lecture, you know, same old shit. Professor Meyerson was up there droning away about something idiotic, as usual, and we were all sitting around falling asleep, as usual, and I started to watch him carefully, really carefully for the first time. I mean, we all know he's a prick, right. But I suddenly realized; he thinks we're a bunch of pricks too. This whole room full of people just . . . what the fuck are we all doing here, that's all I want to know. Four years and I still can't figure it out. Tell me, seriously, I'd really like to know. In twenty-five words or less. No, no, sorry, come on, carnival time, let's go marching.

KATHY. I found it, Bob.

BOB. What?

KATHY. The letter. You left it on the desk.

BOB. (*Puzzled.*) What letter, what are you talking about?

KATHY. (*Pulls an official-looking letter out of her pocket.*) We're supposed to be like all together in here. Why couldn't you just tell us?

BOB. What? Oh no . . . no, Kathy, no . . . (BOB *is laughing faintly at the fact that* KATHY *thinks the letter is what he was trying to tell them about.*) . . . that letter's got nothing to do with anything, and it's none of your business and would you please just give it back . . . ? (*Tries to take it but she holds it away defiantly, and hands it to* RUTH. RUTH *looks at it.*)

RUTH. Woops.

BOB. It's just for a physical. I forgot to register. Look, all I have to do is go down to the . . . oh, Jesus, Kathy . . . (RUTH *has handed the letter on. It goes from hand to hand and ends up with* MIKE. BOB *explains to* MIKE.) I'm not dead yet.

MIKE. They misspelled your name.

BOB. (*Has been pondering something which he finds privately amusing.* MIKE'S *line brings him out of it.*) What?

MIKE. Jobert.

BOB. Oh, yeah.

MIKE. Jobert Rettie. "Dear Jobert Rettie." Hi, Jobert.

BOB. Hi, Jike.

MIKE. Good old Jobert.

COOTIE. How ya feelin', good old Jobert?

BOB. Fine, Jel, sort of dead.

COOTIE. What?

(BOB *laughs at* COOTIE'S *confusion.* MIKE *sees what's happening and comes to the rescue.*)

MIKE. Hi, Jel.

COOTIE. Hi, Jike.

MIKE. Hi, Jorman.

NORMAN. Huh?

MIKE. Hi, Jorman.

NORMAN. Oh, hi.

MIKE. Hi, Jathy, hi, Jick.

DICK. Fuck off.

MIKE. Juck off, why should I juck off, Jick?

(*The DOORBELL RINGS.* COOTIE *rushes over and an-*

answers it. At the door stands RALPH, *a young man in a suit and tie and horn-rimmed glasses. His attaché case is concealed from view outside the door.* COOTIE *is suddenly very serious and low key. In fact, they all calm down. Something new.*)

COOTIE. Hello.

MIKE. Ask him his name, Jel.

COOTIE. What's your name?

RALPH. Ralph.

COOTIE. Hi, Jalph, I'm Jel and that's Jathy, Jorman, Jick, Jike, Juth and Job and we're just on our way down to city hall to beat the shit out of some cops. Wanna come?

RALPH. (*A little off-balance for a moment, rallies and goes into his pitch.*) I'm from the University of Buffalo and I'm in the neighborhood doing some market research. You don't mind if I ask you a few questions, do you?

(*This is timed so that by the end of the line he has leaned forward to pick up his attaché case but in the same gesture moved forward well into the room with his head down and forward, a sequence of moves which he has been taught will force the housewife to give ground. But since* COOTIE *merely stands aside, and the others remain motionless, one sees the whole technique out of context. When* RALPH *is well into the room, he senses that he has used more vigorous motion than the situation called for, and straightens himself slowly, taking in the roomful of people around him. They are all smiling politely.*)

MIKE. Hi.

RALPH. Do all you people live here?

MIKE. No, actually. We're just sort of using the place for a few days. This is a fantastic coincidence, by the way, 'cause the guy that lives here, well, he went away to do a series of special guest lectures at the University of Buffalo.

RALPH. Really? No kidding. Hey, that's some coincidence, huh? That's really a fantastic coincidence. Well, ah, here's what I'd like to do. We're doing a survey for a new educational program and I'd just like to interview one of you people. I'll tell you what. I'll just choose one of you at random and . . . hey, you guys all work, don't you? I mean, you're not students or anything?

COOTIE. Well, all except two of us hold various lower level government positions.

RALPH. I see. Are any of you married?

RUTH. I'm married to him (MIKE) and she's married to him (BOB *and* KATHY.)

BOB. As a matter of fact, we're getting a divorce.

RALPH. Oh, I'm very sorry.

BOB. (*Sincere and helpful.*) No, please. It's just that I've been sort of dying for a while, nothing serious, but now it seems that I'm definitely dead more or less, so we'll have to change my name. It's a legal technicality. We'll marry again under my new name. Jobert. (*Pause.*) Job.

RALPH. (*Smiles weakly.* BOB *smiles at him.*) That's . . . ah . . . well, I think maybe I can just skip over some of the standard form. It has a lot of questions about things that don't apply here, children's opinions and schooling . . .

MIKE. I have several kids by a former marriage.

RUTH. Hey, how come you never told me about that?

MIKE. If you remember, dear, we did discuss it.

RALPH. Can I just edge in here, ha-ha? I mean, I don't want to interrupt a little marital tiff or anything but, ha-ha, you know. (*To* NORMAN.) And how about you, sir, do you have any children?

NORMAN. I don't have any children. I'm not married.

RALPH. Well, sir, I would guess, am I right, I would guess that you are the oldest person staying here. I only mean that in the sense of responsibility. Am I right?

MIKE. The guy that actually lives here is older, but he's not here right now.

RALPH. (*Good-humored.*) No, he's lecturing, right. I remember, ha-ha. Now, I'd just like to ask you the following question. Have you ever heard of a teaching program called the world volumes encyclopedia?

DICK. Hey, are you selling encyclopedias?

RUTH. Hey, yeah, are you trying to sell us a set of encyclopedias?

RALPH. I would like to make it very clear that I am not authorized to sell any product. I'm merely doing market research.

MIKE. Jesus Christ, he's not even selling the fucking things. You go and write to the central office and you wait for a whole year to hear from them and when they finally decide to send a guy around he's not even authorized to sell you a set. Well, I'm not hanging around here listening to some guy who isn't even authorized to sell the World Volumes Encyclopedia while millions of women and children are dying out there in Vietnam. (*Grabs up the banner and walks out singing softly. The others follow.*)

RALPH. (*Yelling after.*) Hey, do you really want to buy a set? I can sell you a set if you really want one. I got a number of special deals . . . and there's a special discount for government employees. (*They're all gone except for* NORMAN. DICK *has gone down the hall to get his coat. To* NORMAN.) Hey, you guys aren't really government employees, are you?

NORMAN. I'm a graduate student.

RALPH. Yeah, well, I didn't want to say anything, but I didn't really think you were government employees. What are you studying?

NORMAN. Mathematics.

RALPH. Oh, man, I wanted to study math. My father wouldn't pay so I'm studying law. Boy, do I hate law. You guys all live together?

NORMAN. Yes.

RALPH. And the girls too?

NORMAN. Yes.

RALPH. Oh, boy, what a life, huh? I'm gonna get me a car pretty soon. I'm saving up. The thing is, I'm having a lot of trouble selling these things. I can't seem to give the sales pitch credibility, and that's pretty bad if I'm gonna be a lawyer, because a lot of the time you have to defend people who you know all along are guilty. The thing is, these encyclopedias are really hard to sell 'cause they cost too much. And they're shitty.

(DICK *re-enters ready for the march, carefully groomed and wearing a pea jacket and well-laundred jeans.*)

DICK. You ready?
NORMAN. Yes.

(DICK *and* NORMAN *start out.* RALPH *is confused.*)

RALPH. Hey, ah, are you going out?
DICK. Listen, if you're gonna eat anything, lay off the hamburgers, okay?
NORMAN. (*While exiting.*) Hey, why's Bob so upset about that letter? Can't he just get a deferment? I've heard of guys that . . .

(DICK *and* NORMAN *are gone.* RALPH *goes to the door, baffled, and looks out. He turns back and sees the empty room.*)

RALPH. Hey.

END OF SCENE TWO

ACT ONE

SCENE 3

A few hours later.

KATHY *is sitting at the table, staring blankly ahead. The front door opens.* RUTH *comes back, her clothes from the previous scene slightly scuffed.* RUTH *sees that* KATHY *is upset.*

RUTH. Hey, what's wrong? Bob here?

KATHY. No.

RUTH. Want some coffee.

KATHY. Please.

RUTH. (*Takes off her coat and starts making coffee.*) I thought you and Bob were coming. You were on the bus and everything. I got lost when the cops charged. Man, they really got some of those guys.

KATHY. When we got there he said he didn't feel like marching.

RUTH. Why not?

KATHY. Oh, Ruthie, I don't know. I don't know anything any more. You devote two years to a guy and what does he give you? He didn't even tell me about being drafted.

RUTH. He's not drafted. For chissakes, Kathy, that letter's for the physical, that's all. All he has to do is act queer. They're not gonna take a queer musician.

KATHY. That's what I told him on the bus. He wouldn't even listen to me until I called him Job. He said from now on he's dead, Bob is dead and everybody has to call him Job.

RUTH. Oh, come on, Kathy, he's just putting you on.

KATHY. That's what I mean. *Me.* He's even putting *me* on. Ungrateful bastard. After all the things I've done for him. (*Pause.*) Shit, I sound just like my mother. It's just you get tired of giving all the time and nothing's coming back. You know what I told him? I said he was the first guy I ever had an orgasm with. I mean, it really made him feel good. Now I gotta live with it.

RUTH. Hey, for real, is he really worried about that letter?

KATHY. He says he's gonna try to pass.

RUTH. What!?

KATHY. He wants to join. That's what he told me. He wants to study engineering in the army and when he gets out he's gonna get some kind of plastic job and marry a nice little plastic wife and live in a plastic house in some plastic suburb and have 2.7 plastic children.

RUTH. Bullshit.

KATHY. Ruthie, I'm telling you, he's serious. Yon know what he told me? He thinks the whole antiwar movement is a goddamn farce. That's what he said. I mean, Jesus, I really thought we were relating on that one. It's not like I'm asking the guy to go burn himself or anything. It's just, I mean, he knows how I feel about this war and he's just doing it to be shitty. I know what it is. He's, like, reaching out, trying to relate to me on a personal level by rejecting me but, like, I don't know how to break through. Oh, Ruth, it's all too much. He went to a cowboy film.

RUTH. Well, you know, that's how it is.

KATHY. Ruthie!

RUTH. Well, I mean, you know, like maybe he's serious. Mike's got this thing about physics. He really digs it and his advisor says he's a genius, okay, maybe he is, like what do I know about physics? The thing is, he knows he's gonna end up working for his old man in the lumber business. It's all laid out from the start. You have to just sort of fit in.

KATHY. You don't want him to do that, do you? I mean, if the guy is really into physics you have to stand behind him and make it all happen for him.

RUTH. I don't know. You have some kids and everything. I mean, it's not like you can't have a meaningful life if you get married and have kids. Look, I don't want the guy to saw wood for the rest of his life but what can I do about it? Why shouldn't he get into wood? Like, what if he does physics for the rest of his life and he's a genius and ends up head of department at some asshole university. You find out one day he's being financed by the C.I.A.

KATHY. These guys. They think they don't need you so you go away and they fall to pieces. You should've seen Bob when I first met him.

RUTH. I did.

KATHY. He used to compose all this really shitty music and like when he did something good he didn't even know it. I had to keep telling him yes, it's good, it's really great. A whole year it took him to believe it. He's writing some brilliant stuff now, ever since, you know, I told him he was the first guy.

RUTH. Yeah, and look at him now.

KATHY. (*Weeping.*) I don't know. You think you're really relating like crazy and then, suddenly, it's a whole new scene.

RUTH. Maybe you ought to stop relating so hard.

(MIKE *bursts in through the front door.*)

MIKE. Holy shit. Where were you?

RUTH. I got lost and came home.

MIKE. Christ, it was horrible.

RUTH. What happened?

MIKE. We got stopped by this line of cops. Me and Cootie were right up front so I told him we should get everyone to join hands and stand still. So we just stood there, you know, and this one dumb pig went apeshit and started running towards Cootie. Well, you know how Cootie always gets diarrhea when he sees pigs. I don't know, I guess he should of said something but he got the urge so bad he just started to run, you know, trying to find a toilet and this dumb pig thought he was trying to resist arrest.

KATHY. Is he all right?

MIKE. The say he'll be O.K. They had to take him to the hospital. He got it in the back.

(COOTIE *walks in.*)

COOTIE. Boy, what a shitty march. You had to go and get separated with all the eats. I could've really used a chunky and marmalade.

RUTH. Hey, listen, Kathy just told me Bob is gonna really go into the army. He's not even gonna try and get out. You know he didn't even go to the march.

COOTIE. He didn't miss much.

KATHY. He went to a goddamn cowboy film.

COOTIE. Hey, is that the one with Kirk Douglas and Gina Lollobrigida and Orson Welles and Tom Courtenay and Kurt Jurgens and . . .

KATHY. You guys are really something. You don't give a shit what happens to him. I thought we were, like, all together in here. Smug bastards.

RUTH. Kathy.

KATHY. I'll tell you something.

COOTIE. What's that, Kathy?

KATHY. You're no better than the people fighting this war. (*Storms out of the room and down the hall. The others sit motionless.*)

MIKE. She's pretty cut up, huh?

RUTH. She thinks he's serious.

MIKE. Isn't he? (*With no warning* COOTIE *jumps up and sings grotesquely, punctuating each beat with a leap into the air. He snarls the song:*)

COOTIE.

WE SHALL OVERCU-U-UM.

WE SHALL OVERCU-U-UM.

WE SHALL OVERCOME SOME DAY-AY-AY-AY-
     AY.

OH-OH-OH, DEEP IN MY HEART

I DO BELIEVE . . .

MIKE. Shut up, Mel.

COOTIE. (*Stopping.*) I'm just protesting the war for Bob. Didn't I stop it? Isn't it over yet?

(DICK *comes in, livid.*)

DICK. Fucking Norman is fucking out of his fucking mind. That's the last time I ever take him with me.

(DICK *takes some milk out of the fridge, kills the bottle and places it on the stack while . . .*)

MIKE. What's the matter, Dick, didn't you get yourself some left-wing ass?

COOTIE Yeah, don't be ashamed, sonny. No need to hide her out there in the hallway. Bring it in and show us the goods.

DICK. Norman brought a gun with him. He took a fucking revolver to the march.

MIKE. Is he a good shot?

DICK. We're sitting on the bus and he's telling me he's reading Ho Chi Min on guerrilla war and he doesn't think marches are effective. So he says he's gonna use the marchers like an indigenous population and start a guerrilla war against the cops. I mean, I thought he was just fucking around. You know Norman. There he pulls out this fucking revolver right there on the bus, people looking and everything and he says he's gonna get a few cops and would I help him create a diversion. He's crazy.

MIKE. How many'd he get?

DICK. Fuck you.

COOTIE. Norman got the girl, huh?

DICK. Where's Kathy and Bob?

RUTH. Bob's not here.

DICK. Kathy here?

RUTH. Leave her alone. She's upset.

COOTIE. Yeah, I wouldn't try to lay her just yet 'cause she's still going with Bob.

(DICK *walks out down the hall.*)

MIKE. That was a pretty stupid thing to say.

COOTIE. Just came out.

RUTH. Who cares? Everyone knows what dirty Dick's up to. Except maybe Bob.

MIKE. And maybe Kathy.

RUTH. Kathy knows.

COOTIE. Do you think a guy could become a homosexual just by willpower?

(*A knock on the front door.*)

RUTH. Come in.

(*In walks* LUCKY, *the downstairs neighbor, led by* MR. WILLIS, *the landlord.*)

WILLIS. Lucky tells me there's been a lotta noise up here. Is that right?

MIKE. Sorry, Mr. Willis, we had a little outburst up here. It's my fault. I just got a letter my sister had a baby.

COOTIE. We were celebrating.

WILLIS. That's all right, but keep it down. Lucky here was saying how you woke his wife up. She's a very ill person. I don't want any more complaints.

LUCKY. Listen, I told you kids once before, and I'm not telling you again. You gotta get rid of those galvanized aluminum garbage cans in the yard and get plastic ones like everyone else.

RUTH. Listen, I don't see why we can't keep the ones . . .

MIKE. Ruth, now calm down, Ruth. I'm sorry, Lucky, but Ruth's pretty upset. Her father's fallen ill and they don't know for sure if it's . . . you know.

LUCKY. You got the galvanized aluminum out there. You'll have to get rid of the galvanized aluminum ones and get plastic.

WILLIS. I'll take care of the rest, Lucky. Thank you for bringing this particular grievance to my attention.

LUCKY. I'll give you 'til Monday, then I want to see plastic out there. (*Leaves.*)

WILLIS. Whew, I hope I seen the last of that loonie today. Nothin' but complaints day and night. The guy was born with a hair across his ass. So who's gonna give the landlord a little coffee? (RUTH *makes a move to get it.*) Thanks, sweetheart. Brother, what a day, what a stinker of a day. Where's Bobby?

MIKE. He's dead.

WILLIS. Dead? He's dead? You guys really kill me, you guys. Yo got a whole sense of humor like nothin' else. Dead, huh? Smart kid, Bobby. Hey, you been to the march?

COOTIE. Yep.

WILLIS. Great march. I watched it on channel eight in color. Brother, clothes you guys wear come out really good on color T.V. You know, that guy Lucky can be a lotta trouble. He got a mind, like, you know, the size of a pinhead, you know what I mean. Just one sugar, sweetheart.

MIKE. You want the rent?

WILLIS. Rent, schment. I come to see how you guys are getting along and you talk to me about rent. How many landlords care, tell me that? One in a million, I can tellya. Hey. You decided whatya gonna do when you get out of college?

COOTIE. I'm gonna be a homosexual.

WILLIS. A homo . . . You guys really slay me, you guys. What a sense of humor. You know, I'd give tena my other tenants for any one of you guys. You kids are the future of America, I mean that deeply, not too much milk, beautiful. Yeah, you kids live a great life up here. I got tenants complaining all the time about the way you kids carry on, and I'll tell you something, you wanna know why they complain? Cause they'd give the last piece of hair on their heads to live like you kids are living.

Ruth. How's Mrs. Willis?

Willis. Huh? Oh, yeah, great, just great. Well, just between you and me and the wall she's gettin' to be a pain in the ass. She wants me to get rid of you too. Why? I ask her. She don't like the way you live. Okay, I say, if you know so much, how do they live? She don't know and she don't wanna know. I try to tell her, you know, about the wild parties and stuff and taking drugs to have all new sensations in the body and the orgies with six or seven of you all at once. You should see her eyes light up. Same thing with all the tenants. When they hear what it's really like up here they go all funny. They'd pay me a hunnerd dollars to hear more but they ain't got the nerve to ask. Get rid of them. That's all I hear. Wamme to tell you something?

Mike. If you got something to say you didn't ought to hold back.

Willis. Tremendous. You kids are tremendous. Listen. When the neighbors try to tellya about when they was young don't believe it. It's a lotta bull, and I should know. When we was young it was so boring you fell asleep when you was twenty and you never woke up again. You hear them stories Lucky tells about the war? Crap. He's sittin' down there holdin' his drink and watchin' Doris Day on television. He'd give his left nut to know what's happenin' up here. This is the best cup of coffee I've had all day. I got a theory about it. It's when the head and the stomach don't talk to each other no more. That's when everything goes to hell. I'm getting so I don't know what I want half the time. I got these dreams, really crazy dreams. I got this one where I'm in a clearing, you know, it's right in the middle of the jungle and there's this tribe of Africans, I mean, like I don't know if they're Africans but they're livin' in the jungle and they're black so I figure they must be Africans. They got this skin, it's you know, black, but really black. This maybe sounds kind of screwy but it's really beautiful this skin. It's a dream, remember. I'm not sayin' black skin is beautiful, if you see what I mean. I'm in charge of the whole works in this jungle and I got it all organized so the men live in one hut and the women live in another hut and there's a big sort of square in between where nobody's allowed after lights out. They live like this all their life. There's no marrying or anything. I'm a kind of witch doctor and I got this tribe believing . . . well, you know, they're just, like, Africans, and they don't know you gotta have a man and a woman to make babies and I got 'em thinkin' you get babies when the moon shines down a girl's "who-jer-ma jiggit" and hits the inside of her womb. And I got this whole ceremony where a girl comes to me when she wants a baby and I tell her she gotta wait until it gets dark and the moon comes up. Then I tie her to a plank, face up and tilt the plank so her thing is facing the moon and then I go to the hut with the guys inside and get one of them to jerk-off on a leaf, you know, one of them tropical leafs that's really big. Then I roll this leaf up like it's a tube and I sneak across the square holding this leaf in my hand all rolled up until I get to the girl. She's lying there in the moonlight all black and shiny and her thing is opened right up 'cause she thinks . . . and I got this tube full of jiz in my hand, and I'm coming closer so I can smell everything and . . . (*Comes out of it.*) Jesus, what am I saying! I'm going crazy. It's just a dream what I'm telling you.

RUTH. That's the most beautiful thing I ever heard.

WILLIS. Listen, I got carried away. I didn't mean none of that.

MIKE. Mr. Willis, if you'd've had the opportunities we've had you'd've probably ended up one of the great poets of the century, and I mean that includes Rimbaud, Rilke, Williams, Pasternak and Ginsberg.

COOTIE. And Whitman.

MIKE. Yes, Whitman included.

WILLIS. Oh Jesus, you kids, you kids. I feel like I can

tell you anything. Somebody could've thought I was pretty screwy if I told them some of them things.

RUTH. You're a beautiful person, Mr. Willis. Never be ashamed of it.

WILLIS. No, I ain't. I ain't ashamed of myself. Hey, I gotta run now. Listen, you know what I was saying about them compliants. I lost a lotta tenants on account of you and I can't afford any more so keep it down.

MIKE. Right.

WILLIS. Or, I'll have to get rid of you. That was wonderful coffee, sweetheart. Thanks, huh. I'll see ya. (*Leaves. There's a slight pause.*)

RUTH. I wonder how long before they put him away.

(KATHY *enters from hall. She moves quickly away from the doorway, tidying her rumpled clothes.* DICK *follows into the room, but stops abruptly when he sees others in the kitchen. He tries to button his shirt casually.*)

COOTIE. Hi, Dick, how's it hanging?

(KATHY *tenses over by the sink.* DICK *turns and goes down the hall.*)

MIKE. I still can't figure out what to get good old Bob for Christmas.

(*Before* KATHY *can reply, the DOORBELL RINGS. No one moves.*)

COOTIE. Whose turn is it?

KATHY. You're a miserable bastard.

COOTIE. What'd I say? We're just playing a chess tournament.

KATHY. Listen, this is my scene, mine. You guys stay out of it, okay, Ruth!

RUTH. It's her scene, guys, you stay out of it.

COOTIE. Roger.

MIKE. Sam.

COOTIE. Larry.

MIKE. Richard.

COOTIE. What's Richard getting Bob for Christmas?

(*The DOORBELL RINGS again, and* MIKE *jumps up to get it.* SHELLY'S *standing there.*)

MIKE. Hello there, I don't know you.

SHELLY. Hi. Does Norman live here?

MIKE. Does anyone here know a Norman?

SHELLY. He said he lived here. I met him at the march today. He said to come here and wait for him. I been standing out in the hall 'cause, like, I heard someone talking and I didn't want to disturb anyone and then this guy came out so I figured, well, it's now or never kind of thing. I'm Shelly.

RUTH. Come on in. I'm Ruth.

SHELLY. Oh, good, then Norman does live here because I wasn't sure when he gave me the address. Sometimes you meet a guy at a march and he'll like give you an address and you end up waiting for a few days and he never shows. Did that ever happen to you? It's happened to me a lot of times.

KATHY. Listen, everyone, I'm serious, I don't want him to know. I'll tell him when the time's right.

RUTH. It's your scene.

(KATHY *exits down hall.* SHELLY *meanwhile goes under the table and sits.*)

SHELLY. I'm sorry about this. If you want to laugh go ahead. I'm used to it. It's just I've got this thing at the moment where I keep sitting under tables and I figured I'd better do it right away instead of pretending for a while I didn't sit under tables. I mean, sitting under the table is "me" at the moment, so why hide it. Have you ever done it?

RUTH. Want some coffee, Shelly?

SHELLY. I'm a vegetarian.

MIKE. Coffee's made from vegetables.

SHELLY. I don't drink coffee, thanks. I'll just wait for Norman.

COOTIE. Where's Norman?

SHELLY. Well, he was arrested for carrying a concealed weapon, but he said it's okay because he has a permit. He's really a total action freak, and he's very committed to the whole peace thing.

COOTIE. Oh.

MIKE. Well now.

COOTIE. How about that.

FADE OUT

END OF SCENE THREE

ACT ONE

SCENE 4

KATHY *is standing and watching* RUTH, *who empties some food scraps from a No. 10 can onto a dish on the floor.*

RUTH. Pwwwwwwsk. Here, kitty-kitty-kitty. Food-food. Chompie—chompie. It's free.

KATHY. (*Has obviously been talking for a while. She continues.*) I never slept with Dick, though. I know you got the idea I did but it's not true. He never got all the way . . .

RUTH. Okay.

KATHY. . . . yet. I'm not saying I wouldn't like to.

RUTH. So go ahead. Pwwwwwwsk, kitty, kitty.

KATHY. Look, don't try to pretend it doesn't mean anything to you. You know as well as I do it'll kill Bob if he ever finds out I'm ever thinking of sleeping with Dick.

RUTH. That's how it goes.

KATHY. Ruthie, look, we've known each other for a long time, right? I can tell when you're thinking something. Now come on, this is a really big decision I gotta make. What am I gonna do about Bob? I mean, it feels like maybe we're, you know, finished, but I like the guy. I really like him a lot and I respect his music. But I know he could never relate to me as a friend. It's gotta be tied up with sex. I mean, Richard really seems to dig me, but I don't know. He's pretty together. He's not the kind of guy you could really do something big for. Not like Bob.

RUTH. Oh, for Christ's sake, Kathy, Dick is a parasite.

KATHY. That's not fair, Ruth.

RUTH. Fair! Do you know what that guy's doing to get into graduate school? You ever heard of Professor Roper in the Eastern Studies department?

KATHY. He's Dick's advisor.

RUTH. Yeah, and he also happens to be queer as a three-dollar bill and Dick is fucking his wife to keep her quiet so good old Roper can suck-cock with all those graduate students from Thailand or Malaya or whatever the hell they are.

KATHY. Who said?

RUTH. Who said? For chrissakes, Kathy, the whole Goddamn school knows about it. Dirty Dicky.

KATHY. That's why?

RUTH. Yeah, what else? I mean, the guy washes eight times a day.

KATHY. Oh, man, how long have you guys known about this? I mean, like, why didn't anyone ever tell me? You can't just let him screw up his future like that. Hasn't anyone tried to do anything about it?

RUTH. Like tell him Mrs. Roper's got clap?

KATHY. Ruthie, the guy must be really suffering.

RUTH. Oh shit, Kathy, let's not have the big savior thing.

KATHY. That's not very funny.

RUTH. Look, we're all gonna graduate pretty soon, and we're all gonna go away and probably we'll never see each other again except maybe like at Christmas or something. So why don't you worry about yourself and never mind about Dick and Bob? They'll be okay.

KATHY. Boy, you sure have changed, Ruth. I don't know. You sure have changed.

(BOB *comes through front door with books.*)

BOB. I don't believe it. It's incredible. You know what happened today in counterpoint class? Remember I was telling you about Eric Shatz?

RUTH. . . . three armpits . . . ?

BOB. The very one.

KATHY. (*Nicely.*) Bob . . .

BOB. (*Who has gone to the icebox to steal some of* DICK's *hamburgers, stops short in whatever gesture he is holding, only for a moment though, just long enough to cut* KATHY. *When he resumes his story, he is talking only to* RUTH, *who is now wrapping a Christmas present.*) Today, Shatz turned in this perfect, spotless clean counterpoint exercise. I mean, for someone as filthy as Shatz, that's a miracle. (BOB *has the hamburgers out by now.* KATHY, *being all nice, takes the hamburgers from him, indicating that she'll cook.* BOB *goes away from her and sits with* RUTH.) He picks his nose and squeezes his pimples right there in class, and his counterpoint exercises have to be seen to be believed. He writes them in pencil, and if he makes a mistake or something, he spits on his eraser and rubs the paper about a hundred times . . . per note, so by the time he hands it to Professor Bolin, it's just this gray sludge with lots of little black things swimming around on it. Anyway, about a week ago, when Shatz handed over his work, Professor Bolin put on a pair of gloves before he'd take it, so Shatz must've got the message and this week when Bolin called for homework, Shatz set this beautiful clean exercise down on the piano. We couldn't believe it. Bolin just sat there staring at it, and we all sat staring at Bolin and after about ten minutes, no shit, it took that long, Bolin turned to us and said, "Free will is an illusion." Isn't that too much?

KATHY. Bob, can I talk to you . . . ?

BOB. (*Ignores her.*) The thing is, Bolin's got a Ph.D. He's also written two books and a couple of hundred symphonies and string quartets and they say he taught himself twenty-two languages in four hours or something. . . .

KATHY. Please, Bob, I want to talk to you. . . .

BOB. And another thing, Bolin's wife got drunk at a faculty party for the music department last year and she yelled, "Fuck Schoenberg, I get it off with Miles Davis," and then she went and laid the only black professor in the school, which all goes to show that when Bolin tells you free will is an illusion . . . you better believe it.

KATHY. (*Pointed.*) Bob, I would like to talk to you. . . .

BOB. Hey, Ruth, did I ever tell you the one about the guy that died and came back to life as Job?

KATHY. Oh, don't start that shit again.

BOB. Again? It started over a month ago. I mean, even Bolin caught on after two lessons. Of course he still makes me walk around the music building every time I put down parallel fifths, but that's how it goes, life is trying at the best of times, every cloud has a silver lining, a stitch in time saves nine. . . .

RUTH. (*Looks at her watch.*) I've gotta go.

BOB. Did I say something?

RUTH. No. Kathy wants to talk to you about sleeping with Dick.

KATHY. Ruth . . . bitch!

(RUTH *goes out the front door, grabbing her coat on the way.*)

BOB. (*Pause.*) You'll never believe this, but when I came in just now, I didn't expect that. Bedbugs, maybe. Thermonuclear war. . . .

KATHY. She had no right.

BOB. I'm trying to think of something appropriate to say, like "Name the first one after me." That's Job. J-O-B. Job.

KATHY. Please, Bob, can I say something . . .

BOB. Do you have trouble pronouncing the name "Job"?

KATHY. Jesus Christ, you're impossible.

BOB. Ah, yes, but I exist, nonetheless.

KATHY. You've just cut me right out. You're not even trying to relate to me any more. (*Pause.*) Well, you're not.

BOB. No, Kathy. The fact is, I like you a lot. I, um, sort of love you, if you know what I mean.

KATHY. I don't really want to sleep with Dick.

BOB. Then don't.

KATHY. It's just, he tried to get me that night after the demonstration.

BOB. I know. He told me.

KATHY. That shit.

BOB. I thought it was pretty good of him.

KATHY. He never got into me, you know.

BOB. That's nice.

KATHY. Oh, Bob, I'm sorry.

BOB. If Bob were around I'm sure he'd forgive you.

KATHY. What'll we do?

BOB. What do you mean? Like study or something?

KATHY. Bob, how does it stand? Is it . . . it's over, isn't it?

BOB. Between us, you mean?

KATHY. Yes.

BOB. If that's what you want.

KATHY. Of course I don't want it. I love you a lot.

BOB. O.K. So let's study for Phil 540.

KATHY. Oh for chrissakes show some emotion. I don't know where I'm at with you half the time.

BOB. Look, what's the big hang-up? If you want to stay with me, okay. If you want to move into Dick's room, go ahead. If you don't know for sure, stay one night with me and one night with him until you start feeling a definite preference for one of us . . .

KATHY. Jesus Christ, what's the matter with you, Bob?

BOB. I'm Job. Bob's dead.

KATHY. (*Is in a furious slow burn. She stands and goes toward the hall door.*) All right . . . all right. . . .

(*Before she can exit a knock on the door stops her. A game. Who's going to open the door. BOB picks up a book and starts reading. Another knock. KATHY sighs. She's above these silly games. She opens the door on a middle-aged man in well-cut coat. A businessman from head to foot. This is MURRY, BOB's uncle.*)

MURRY. Hi. Does Bob Rettie live here?

(KATHY *steps back and* BOB *looks up from his book.*)

BOB. Murry!!

MURRY. (*Smile.*) Can I come in?

BOB. (*Standing.*) What the hell are you doing here?

MURRY. Guy flies a couple thousand miles to see his nephew, maybe he can come in, huh?

BOB. Yeah, yeah. Come in, come in . . . sit down . . .

MURRY. Hey, I bet you're surprised to see me, huh? Maybe a little happy.

BOB. Yeah, I mean I haven't seen you for a couple thousand years or something.

MURRY. (*To* KATHY.) It's longer than that since he wrote.

BOB. Oh, ah, that's Kathy. My uncle.

MURRY. How do you do.

KATHY. Hi.

MURRY. You drink a lot of milk, huh?

BOB. Yeah.

(*They look at each other and laugh.*)

MURRY. Where'd you get that goddamn icebox?

BOB. Oh, you know . . .

MURRY. Is this the way you been living? Bobby boy, why didn't you tell me. Write a letter, say Murry I need a little cash, I'd've sent you some money for a decent refrigerator.

BOB. Murry, we're living O.K.

MURRY. So. I'm sorry for breathing. Did I interrupt something?

BOB. No. Nothing at all.

MURRY. Are you two . . . ah . . .

BOB. (*Quickly.*) Yeah—Murry look, sit down, take your coat off . . .

MURRY. (*Smiles at* BOB. *He's an old sport. He knows the score.*) Hey, Bobby, Bobby-boy. You got long hair . . .

BOB. Yeah, it keeps growing.

MURRY. Still proud, huh? (*To* KATHY.) Just like his mother. . . . (MURRY *looks at the two of them and shrugs* . . .) Well, what can I say . . .

KATHY. Look, I think I'll . . .

BOB. (*Cutting in.*) How long you in town for?

MURRY. Oh, you know. Business.

KATHY. Excuse me, I'm gonna . . .

BOB. (*Cutting in.*) How's the kids?

MURRY. Oh, fine, fine, keep asking about you.

BOB. Auntie Stella?

MURRY. Oh. You know. We got a new house . . .

BOB. Great. Where you going, Kathy . . . ?

KATHY. (*Has been edging toward the door. Quietly.*) I'll be in Dick's room if you want me.

MURRY. Hey look, maybe I should . . .

BOB. No, Murry, it's O.K. Come on, Kathy, you can stay for a minute . . . he's my uncle, he wants to get to know the girl I'm going to marry. . . .

KATHY. (*Is stunned. This, more than anything, hits her where she lives.*) What?!

BOB. Didn't I write you about that, Murry? I thought I wrote you about how I met this fantastic girl . . . oh, I probably didn't tell you her name . . . yeah, we're getting married right after graduation, isn't that right, Kathy . . . ?

(KATHY *is too stunned to speak.*)

MURRY. (*Amazed.*) What can I say, I don't know what to say . . .

BOB. (*Takes* KATHY's *limp hand in what looks like an affectionate gesture but mainly to hold her there . . .*) Oh, yeah, we're gonna have kids and settle down and everything but we have to wait a little bit because I'm still pretty messed up but Kathy's done wonderful things for me and with a little more help I'll be all ready for the big step. . . .

KATHY. (*Her eyes are closed.*) Let go of my hand, Bob. (*He does. She walks out quietly.* MURRY *stares after her.* BOB *stares at* MURRY.)

MURRY. Is she O.K.?

BOB. (*Flat.*) Yeah. It's her time of the month, you know.

MURRY. Say no more. You don't have to tell me about that. Nice girl. Very nice. (*Laughs.*) So . . .

BOB. Come through New York?

MURRY. Yeah, you know, passed through.

BOB. You passed through New York, huh?

MURRY. (*Uneasy.*) Yeah, sure, you know . . .

BOB. D'you see mom?

MURRY. Yeah, I dropped by, you know.

BOB. How is she, Murry?

MURRY. She's fine. Fine. Hey, she didn't say anything about . . . Didn't you tell her yet?

BOB. Not yet.

MURRY. You should tell her soon.

BOB. Why should I tell her soon, Murry . . . ?

MURRY. Well, I mean, you know, your own mother . . .

BOB. (*Kicks a chair or something.* . . .) We've been sort of keeping it secret, Murry, you know what I mean. . . .

MURRY. (*Confused.*) Bobby . . .

BOB. Just one of those stupid secrets, one of those dumb fucking secrets like the one you've been keeping from me for two years. . . .

MURRY. What?

BOB. It was two years ago, wasn't it, that first operation? Kidney trouble. Shit. How is she, Murry? How's good old Mom that you just dropped by to see on your way here?

MURRY. (*Stands   dumbly,   arms   outstretched.*) Bobby . . .

BOB. (*Taunting.*) What is it, cancer? (*Pause.*) How long's she got?

MURRY. (*Broken.*) A week. Two weeks. They don't know. . . .

BOB. Why didn't someone tell me?

MURRY. You had your studies, we should worry you to death . . . ?

BOB. Did you ever think I might've liked to know something like that two years ago? Didn't anyone realize I'd like to have known that my own mother was dying . . .

MURRY. (*Comes to comfort* BOB.) Bobby . . .

BOB. Bob . . . and fuck you all. (*Moves away from* MURRY *and leaves him stranded.*)

MURRY. I thought you and me . . . we maybe fly to New York tonight.

BOB. Yeah. Get in there quick for the payoff. That'll be just great.

MURRY. She doesn't know yet. . . .

BOB. Yeah, "Hi, Mom, just came flying in with Murry a couple weeks before Christmas vacation to see you for no good reason." You think she won't guess?

MURRY. She doesn't have to. We can always tell her something.

BOB. Another big secret, huh, Murry? It's gotta be the first thing she thought of. Two years. She's been dying for two years and I didn't even fucking know it. . . .

MURRY. I don't want to hurt anybody.

BOB. I'll pack some stuff. No. You stay in here. I want to be alone.

(BOB *exits down the hall. Immediately* MURRY *pulls a half quart bottle of whiskey out of his inner pocket. It's wrapped in a paper bag. He fumbles the cap off and drinks deeply.* MIKE *and* COOTIE *enter from outside, laden with presents. They cross the room slowly, looking at* MURRY *who hides his bottle.* MIKE *and* COOTIE *exit and a furious debate follows offstage. They enter seconds later and cross to* MURRY *deferentially.*)

MIKE. Me and my friend were wondering if you could settle a little argument for us.

MURRY. What?

MIKE. Were you or weren't you the guy behind the bar in *Key Largo,* starring Humphrey Bogart and Edward G. Robinson?

MURRY. I'm Bob's uncle.

MIKE. (*To* COOTIE.) He's Bob's uncle.

COOTIE. Are you a for-real uncle?

MURRY. (*Confused.*) Yeah, yeah, I'm his uncle.

COOTIE. Maternal or paternal?

MURRY. I'm related to Bob through his mother. She was . . . she's my sister.

MIKE. That's a pretty convincing story, mister.

COOTIE. Most of the pieces fit pretty good.

(MIKE *and* COOTIE *start toward the hall.* SHELLY *comes in the front door.*)

SHELLY. Hi, everyone.
MIKE. Hiya, Shelly.
COOTIE. Good old Shelly, hiya.

(MIKE *and* COOTIE *are gone down the hall.*)

SHELLY. Hey . . . excuse me, do you know if Norman's here?
MURRY. I don't know who Norman is.
SHELLY. One of the guys here. I mean he lives here. You someone's father?
MURRY. I'm Bob's uncle.
SHELLY. Bob? Oh, yeah, Job. (*She sits under the table.*) I'm waiting for Norman. Hey, are you, like, a for-real uncle?
MURRY. You kids keep asking that.
SHELLY. You don't think of him with an uncle.
MURRY. Look, if you don't want me to stay in here, I'll go and help Bob.
SHELLY. No, you stay here. Like, I enjoy company. Hey, is he here?
MURRY. I'm afraid I don't know your friend Norman.
SHELLY. I mean Job. Your nephew.
MURRY. Yes, he's here. I'm waiting for him.
SHELLY. He's like, in here somewhere? Inside the apartment?
MURRY. Yes. Look, you want to go down and ask him about Norman, go ahead.
SHELLY. Is he in the toilet?
MURRY. He's in his room.
SHELLY. Wow, that's, like, really weird.
MURRY. He's just packing, that's all.
SHELLY. Yeah, but I mean, if you're his for-real uncle how come you're like sitting in here when he's down there?

MURRY. Look, he . . . (*Weeping softly.*) . . . I don't know.

SHELLY. Hey, what's the matter? I thought you were, like, waiting for him to come back here, you know, like, to the apartment or something. I just wanted to know because I'm waiting for Norman to come back so I thought we could maybe sit here together waiting and that would be something we had in common . . . then you told me he was in his room packing and everything and I thought that was sort of weird 'cause if you're his for real like you could just go down there and be with him. (*Pause.*) Why's he packing?

BOB. (*Entering with bag.*) O.K., I'm ready.

SHELLY. Hey, Job, you going away?

BOB. I'll be back in a few days.

SHELLY. Like, you mean, you're not just going home early for Christmas vacation?

BOB. No.

SHELLY. Oh. Okay. Hey, Merry Christmas, you guys.

BOB. Merry Christmas.

MURRY. Merry Christmas.

(DICK *comes in through the front door.* BOB *and* MURRY *start out.* DICK *is baffled.*)

DICK. Hey, you going?

BOB. Yeah. Kathy's in your room. (*Pause.*) She doesn't like it from behind. (BOB *and* MURRY *are gone.*)

SHELLY. Man, there's something really weird going on here.

DICK. Where's he going?

SHELLY. I don't know, but the guy with him is his for-real uncle and he's a weird head.

(KATHY *comes into the kitchen.*)

KATHY. Hey, did Bob just go out?

SHELLY. Wow, he didn't even tell you?

DICK. He left with his uncle.

KATHY. Left?

DICK. He had a suitcase.

KATHY. Jesus, why didn't he say something? I mean, I been waiting for him down there . . .

SHELLY. Well, the guy who said he was the uncle said Job went down to his room to pack, and I mean, like if you were in there with him and he started putting a lot of socks and underwear and toilet stuff in a suitcase you should've got suspicious and asked him something, like where's he going.

KATHY. Look, I went to the bathroom, okay?

SHELLY. Ya didn't flush.

KATHY. Mind your own goddamn business, Shelly. What does he expect me to do? How can I make plans for the Christmas vacation if he just . . . shit, he could've said something. (DICK, *in a feeble attempt to avoid* KATHY's *rage, tries to sneak out down the hallway*.) And listen, you, you have a lot of nerve telling him about that night.

DICK. I didn't say anything.

KATHY. He said you told him.

DICK. Honest, Kathy, I never did.

KATHY. (*Vague*.) I'm really getting to hate this place. (*Starts down the hall*. DICK *starts after her*.)

DICK. Kathy!

SHELLY. Dick, have you seen Norman?

DICK. Yeah, I see him every day.

SHELLY. You're a shit, Dick.

(*Before* DICK *can get down the hall*, RUTH *rushes in through the front door, breathless*.)

RUTH. Oh, wow, have I ever had the most fantastic experience. (DICK *goes down the hall, slamming the door. Yelling*.) You're a shit, Dick.

SHELLY. You seen Norman?

RUTH. Oh, hi, Shelly. Hey, let me tell you about what just happened to me. It really blew my mind.

(From down the hall we hear voices singing.)

MIKE *and* COOTIE. *(Singing.)*
> We wish you a Merry Christmas
> We wish you a Merry Christmas
> We wish you a Merry Christmas
> We wish you a Merry Christmas
> We wish you a Merry Christmas
> We wish you a Merry Christmas
> We wish you a Merry Christmas
> We wish you a Merry Christmas . . . and
> (MIKE *and* COOTIE *rush in from the hall dressed in Santa Claus costumes and end the song.)*
> . . . a Happy New Year.

MIKE. We got a present for you, Ruth.

SHELLY. Hey, where'd you get those?

COOTIE. We're doing collections this year. Yep.

MIKE. You want to see the great old present we got ya?

RUTH. I was just gonna tell Shelly what happened when I went to see Quinn. You know Quinn, the albino dwarf . . .

MIKE. Oh, yeah, old Quinn.

COOTIE. Good old Quinn.

RUTH. Yeah, right, well, I had to see him about homework for the Christmas vacation and I mean, like, he was the last person I wanted to see. I always thought he was a vicious little bastard. I mean, he can be pretty shitty.

MIKE. They say he shot a man in Abilene.

COOTIE. In the back.

RUTH. Listen, willya. I went into his office and he's standing by the window, you know, three feet high and everything. I thought he was probably gonna ask why I wasn't doing any homework, and I had this whole speech worked out about how I thought he was a pretentious little snot and how I frankly didn't give a shit about philosophy and even less of a shit about him, if that's possible and . . . oh, you know, I was really going to kill him. Anyway, he told me to come over to the window, so I came over and we both stood there looking out. Snow everywhere, like, white wherever you looked and a lot of snow coming down like in those paperweights you shake up, and there's all these kids down below coming out of the building, all little lumps moving across the white in slow motion, and we're looking at them, just the two of us, for, I don't know, about a minute or two and then he just turns to me, like without any warning, and says this incredibly beautiful thing . . .

MIKE. Hey, don't you want to see the nifty present we got ya?

RUTH. Let me tell you what the guy said, willya?

MIKE. Right, you tell us what Quinn said, then we'll show you the present.

RUTH. Yeah.

MIKE. Will you look at the present first then tell us what Quinn said?

RUTH. For Christ sake stop fucking around and listen.

MIKE. All right, what did Quinn say?

COOTIE. I'd like to hear what Quinn said.

(*As* RUTH *is about to speak,* KATHY *runs through from the hall and out of the front door with a valise in hand.* DICK *shouts from offstage down the hall.*)

DICK. (*Offstage.*) Kathy. (DICK *enters and on his way across the room and out the front door, buttons his overcoat.*) Kathy!

(RUTH's *face shows worry as she watches this. Seconds after* DICK *exits, she takes her coat and follows, leaving* MIKE, COOTIE *and* SHELLY *alone. There is a pause.*)

COOTIE. What was that all about?

MIKE. Things around here are gettin' a little out of control, Cootie.

COOTIE. You feel that way, huh?

MIKE. Yeah, that's right, our uncle's a cop. . . .

NORMAN. That's what I mean, you see.

MIKE. What do you mean?

NORMAN. Well, I mean, you have to go making fun of my father being a cop.

COOTIE. Norman, there are 982,400 policemen in this country. So why the hell should you be the only one around here with a cop in the family?

(*A knock on the door.*)

MIKE. Come in. (*To* NORMAN.) See, we could do . . .

(*Two policemen enter.* BREAM *is elderly.* EFFING *is young.*)

BREAM. (*To* MIKE.) You live here?

MIKE. Yes, sir.

BREAM. Look, you know what I mean, you and who else?

MIKE. Well, there's me and my brother Cootie . . . um, Melvin, and there's Norman, Dick, Jobert and Ruth.

BREAM. Ruth, huh? That's a girl's name.

MIKE. Ruth is a girl, sir.

BREAM. (*To* SHELLY.) You're Ruth, huh?

SHELLY. I'm Shelly.

BREAM. (*To* MIKE.) You didn't say nothing about no Shelly.

MIKE. She doesn't live here, sir.

BREAM. Visiting?

SHELLY. I'm with Norman.

BREAM. You're Norman.

NORMAN. She's my girl friend.

BREAM. Good, we got that figured out.

EFFING. (*Inspecting.*) Hey, Bream, they got a map of Europe.

BREAM. Yeah. Now listen. We got a complaint about

you guys from the people across there. (*Indicates window.*) I know you're students and you probably think you own the God damn country. Well, I got some news for you. There's laws around here and you gotta obey them same as anybody else.

MIKE. I think we all appreciate that fact, sir.

COOTIE. I certainly appreciate it. I think I can speak for Shelly and Norman, and if any of the other guys were in I'm sure they'd appreciate it a lot.

EFFING. Hey, Bream, look at all them milk bottles.

BREAM. Yeah, now listen, I'm gonna say this and I'm only gonna say it once and you're gonna listen careful 'cause I ain't got time for any more compliants about you guys. No . . . more . . . trouble. Understand?

MIKE. Yes, sir.

COOTIE. Yes, sir.

NORMAN. What did we do?

BREAM. What do you mean, what did you do?

NORMAN. Just, you know, I mean, what was the complaint?

BREAM. The compliant was guys and girls parading around in here bare ass. Now look, I'm a reasonable man. I know what I know and I know what I don't know and one of the things I know God damn well I don't know is what the hell you kids are up to now 'days, but O.K. that's my problem, right. And I hope you notice I'm winking one eye when it comes to the law about cohabitation.

MIKE. We noticed that right away, sir. And thank you.

BREAM. O.K.

MIKE. We don't lack appreciation for what's involved in the life of a policeman. For Christ's sake, his father's a cop.

COOTIE. Our uncle's a cop.

MIKE. So it's not like we don't know what you guys gotta put up with. It can be a pretty crabby job.

BREAM. Hey.

MIKE. No, I don't mean it doesn't have its rewards.

His father's very happy in his work. Our uncle's life is very meaningful.

BREAM. (*Suspicious.*) Yeah, that's what I'm talking about.

(COOTIE *is edging toward the hall door.* EFFING *barks.*)

EFFING. Hey, Bream. (BREAM *jumps up and reaches for his gun.* COOTIE *freezes.* BREAM *looks at* EFFING.) The kid's leaving the room.

COOTIE. I got a call from nature.

BREAM. Jesus Christ, Effing, what's the matter with you? Go ahead, kid. (COOTIE *exits.*)

EFFING. Bream, the kid says he's going to the toilet and what if he's got some stuff on him he can just flush it down and come back clean.

BREAM. He's O.K.

EFFING. Jesus, Bream. Sir.

BREAM. Guy's new on the job. He don't know the score yet.

MIKE. I think probably somebody exaggerated, you know, about our being bare ass. People always exaggerate. I mean, look what they say in the papers about you guys. (*Pause.*) Maybe like after a shower or something we'll come in here for an anchovie snack on toast or a chocolate milk and we'll just forget to put something on.

EFFING. Bream, that girl keeps sitting under the table.

BREAM. Goddamn it, Effing, did we come here to investigate a complaint about a girl sitting under a table?

EFFING. No, sir, but—

BREAM. The girl happens to be well within her rights as a taxpaying citizen to sit under any table she wants, and until we get a complaint about her sitting under there we leave her alone.

EFFING. But, sir, the . . .

BREAM. Effing.

EFFING. Sir.

BREAM. Shut up.

EFFING. Yes, sir.

SHELLY. Thanks.

BREAM. That's O.K., lady. The kid's a rookie. Now let me tell you something about the people complaining about you. They look in here and see you guys bare-assed and they're complaining because they're so sick of looking at each other they gotta go spying on you. We know about them people. They're strict Roman Catholic. Twelve kids in four rooms. The old man can't keep it in his pants for ten minutes running. So they got troubles, right, and everyone that's got troubles wants to give troubles to someone else. So they make a complaint, and that's well within their rights as law-abiding citizens of this community. I got enough troubles without their God-damn complaints. I got enough to do watching the Vietnam freaks and the niggers and the loonies going up on buildings with high-power rifles. Let me give you some good advice. Get curtains. They got some fiberglass curtains at Woolworth's you can't tell them from the real cotton. $12.50 a pair and they come in right colors, plain and patterned. You get a rod for $1.75, and for a total of $14.25 you save yourself from a lot of crazy neighbors. If you can't afford $14.25 get some gingham, 39¢ a yard at Penney's. Measure your windows and allow a foot extra at each end. All you gotta do is take up a six-inch hem at each end, fold it over once and hand-stitch. A couple of curtain rings and you're in business. Can you remember that or d'you want me to write it down?

SHELLY. Hey, yeah, would you do that?

(BREAM *takes out a notebook and writes.*)

EFFING. The kid's been gone a long time.

BREAM. I got eyes, Effing. (*To* NORMAN.) Boy, that's really something. Cop sending his kid to college. They must pay him pretty good.

NORMAN. I guess so.

BREAM. Yeah, what's he—sergeant, lieutenant, or something?

NORMAN. He's chief of police. Erie County, New York.

BREAM. Pretty good, that shut me up O.K. chief of police, huh? (*Thinking.*) What's his name?

NORMAN. Max.

(COOTIE *enters hiking up his pants before* BREAM *can respond to* NORMAN.)

COOTIE. That's better.

BREAM. (*Tears out his page of instructions.*) I want to see curtains up there by Wednesday or you'll be in court, father or no father, you understand?

MIKE. Yes, sir.

BREAM. This ain't Erie County. (BREAM *and* EFFING *exit.* MIKE *drifts to the door and listens. He relaxes.*)

SHELLY. Oh, wow.

MIKE. (*Collapses, laughing. So does* COOTIE. *So does* SHELLY. NORMAN *follows suit.* MIKE, *gasping.*) Max!!!

NORMAN. (*Stops laughing.*) That's his name.

MIKE. O.K.

NORMAN. And he is chief of police.

MIKE. We believe you.

NORMAN. Then why do you always have to go making fun of my father?

MIKE. What are you getting all paranoid about? You don't believe our uncle's a cop, do you? (NORMAN *is baffled.*) So why should we believe your father is?

COOTIE. Don't we believe it?

MIKE. (*Calmly.*) Of course we do. Because we trust you, Norman.

COOTIE. And if you'd been a little more generally outer-directed we'd probably have learned about that 38 police special you were toting around last fall.

MIKE. It's definitely not cool to bring guns to a march, Norman; it'll always end in a tragic episode. Permit or no.

COOTIE. As indeed it did.

MIKE. Indeed.

NORMAN. Yeah, well, I don't know about you guys.

MIKE. You're not trying to say that getting kicked out of school wasn't a tragic episode.

COOTIE. It was an abortion of academic freedom, pure and simple.

MIKE. Here, here!

COOTIE. I mean, when they kick mathematics graduate students out of school just for trying to murder a few cops . . . And, by the way, Norman, I've heard that your being kicked out of school was the doing of the Dean of Admissions, a man who is known far and wide to be cornholding his widowed sister in the eye-sockets regularly. . . .

MIKE. And without love.

COOTIE. And when the moon comes up, he ties her to this plank . . .

MIKE. Mel . . .

COOTIE. And don't try to tell us you enjoy having to schlepp down the Hays Bick Cafeteria everynight to wash dishes for a dollar ten an hour.

NORMAN. Oh, I don't know.

SHELLY. Hey, are you guys brothers?

MIKE. Now there. Look at that, Norman. Shelly's wondering about the relationship between Mel and me and instead of being all paranoid about it and going crazy wondering she comes right out and asks.

SHELLY. Hey, are you?

COOTIE. Yeah, we're brothers.

SHELLY. Wow, I didn't know that either. I keep learning all these things about you guys.

MIKE. See, everything's cool now. Everybody trusts each other. That's what it's all about.

NORMAN. Well, I mean, with washing dishes I get more time to read. I've been thinking a lot and I guess it's like Dick said. I was pretty irrelevant before. Mathematics is pretty irrelevant no matter how you look at it, and bad mathematics is about as irrelevant as you can get.

SHELLY. I left school after the first month. I'm not saying I'm really relevant, yet, but like, some of my friends in school are really into bad scenes. School is evil. You can't find out where it's at when you're studying all the time to fit your head into exams. I'm getting to where I can read receipes all day and really get something out of it.

NORMAN. Yeah. I'm learning all this stuff about Vietnam. It's really something. I mean, I'm getting to the point where maybe I can do something really relevant about it.

SHELLY. Norman's got this fantastic idea.

NORMAN. Well, I haven't thought it all out yet . . .

SHELLY. No, Norman-baby, don't like close all up. It's the most relevant thing I ever heard of.

COOTIE. Jesus, Norman, how long have you been walking around with this idea locked up inside you?

NORMAN. I didn't get it all at once. It sort of came in stages but I think it's about right.

COOTIE. Man, you're gonna go crazy if you keep everything inside like that.

SHELLY. Tell them the idea, Norman.

NORMAN. Well . . . (*Pause.*) I'm gonna set myself on fire as a protest against the war. (COOTIE *and* MIKE *look at him and exchange brief glances.*) I've thought about it a lot. I mean, I've read I guess about a hundred books about the war and the more you read the more you see it's no one thing you can put your finger on. Like Dick said. I shouldn't've tried to kill those policemen, but I didn't know then they were part of the system like everything else. No one's got the right to take anyone else's life, that's what I've decided. But I've still got the right to take my own life for something I believe in.

SHELLY. I'm gonna burn with Norman. We're gonna burn together. We've thought it all through and, like, if he burns himself alone that's just one person. Everyone'll say he's insane, but if two of us do it . . . wow. Two people. What are they gonna say if two of us do it?

(*Pause.*)

MIKE. (*Pause.*) Three of us.

COOTIE. Four of us.

MIKE. You, too, huh?

COOTIE. It's the only way.

NORMAN. Hey, wait a minute. I've read a lot about the whole subject and I really know just why I'm gonna do it. I'm not just doing it for fun or anything. You can't just jump into it.

MIKE. Listen, Norman, you don't have to believe this if you don't want to, but it's the truth, on my honor. Me and Cootie talked about the same thing a year ago. We were all ready to burn ourselves . . .

COOTIE. It was more than a year ago.

MIKE. More than a year?

COOTIE. Almost a year and a half.

MIKE. That's right, a year and a half. Boy, time really goes quick.

COOTIE. It sure does.

MIKE. The thing is, we decided against it because we figured two isn't enough.

COOTIE. You know how the papers can lie. "Brothers Burn."

MIKE. Yeah, "Hippie Brothers Suicide Pact." That kind of shit.

COOTIE. Think of it though. With four of us.

NORMAN. You really want to do it?

MIKE. It's the only way.

NORMAN. I mean, I wasn't sure yet. I hadn't made up my mind definitely. I was still looking for another way.

SHELLY. No, Norman-baby, like you said, it's the only relevant gesture.

(*Long pause.*)

NORMAN. Okay.

MIKE. After the Easter vacation.

COOTIE. No, no, after graduation. We'll study like mad and get fantastic grades and graduate with honors, so they can't say we were cracking up or anything.

MIKE. Yeah, we'll get Phi Beta Kappa. I'd like to see them say we're insane when two Phi Beta Kappas go up in flame with the son of a policeman and the daughter of a . . . Hey, what does your father do?

SHELLY. Well, it's kind of weird. He's like . . . (*Lying.*) dead.

MIKE. That's okay, Daughter of a Dead Father. That covers the whole spectrum.

NORMAN. What does you father do? I mean, I know your uncle's a policeman because I trust you, but you never said what your father did. I was curious. Like, if they bring our fathers into it what'll they say about you?

COOTIE. He's a trapper.

SHELLY. Wow, that's really something else. Like, a fur trapper?

COOTIE. Furs and hides, you know. Rabbit and mink and muskrat and beaver and elk and reindeer and seal. Some otter. Penguin.

SHELLY. Wow, penguin.

COOTIE. Well, you know, he works the Great Northwest Territory and up to the mouth of the St. Lawrence seaway and over to the Aleutians.

SHELLY. Boy, this'll really blow everyone's mind.

MIKE. Yeah, this'll make everyone think twice, all right. (SHELLY *and* NORMAN *exit* U. MIKE *and* COOTIE *play chess.*) When the time comes I hope I'll be able to go through with it, Cootie.

COOTIE. What?

MIKE. (*Smiles,* COOTIE *laughs.*) Will you?

END OF SCENE ONE

ACT TWO

Scene 2

Most of the posters are down. A bare feeling. Around graduation. There're some letters on the table.

Ruth, alone, is reading her letter. Dick comes in from outside, dressed for warm weather, perhaps carrying a box. He opens the icebox.

Dick. Shit, nothing left.

Ruth. We cleaned it.

Dick. Anyone gone yet?

Ruth. No. Why don't you look at your grades?

Dick. (*Opens letter.*) Jesus.

Ruth. Bad?

Dick. Fucking awful.

Ruth. Do you graduate?

Dick. Yeah, just.

Ruth. They sent Kathy's grades here.

Dick. That was tactful.

Ruth. Maybe she'll be around to pick them up. I got into graduate school.

Dick. Great.

Ruth. Philosophy.

Dick. Philosophy?

Ruth. Yeah! (*Pause.*) I mean, you know, why not? (Dick *starts toward the hall.*) Hey, Dick, I don't get it. You know that day she left, just before Christmas . . . did you get into her?

Dick. How low can you stoop, Ruth?

Ruth. No, I mean, you know, just, she must've done something to fuck you up this bad.

Dick. Kathy did not fuck me up.

Ruth. Yeah, well, ever since she left you've been looking like really terrible. You never even studied for finals. I mean, you were the academic head around here. Hey, you did get into her, didn't you, and I bet she told you you were the first guy that ever turned her on. (DICK *starts out again.*) Did she? Oh, come off it, Dick, I just . . . I thought we were friends.

DICK. You know what that little bitch told me just before she left? She told me I was screwing Roper's wife. Me, screwing Roper's wife.

RUTH. Well, you know Kathy.

DICK. She said everybody in the whole fucking school knew about it. It got back to Roper.

RUTH. Wow, I bet he was pretty pissed off, huh?

DICK. He was pretty good about it, considering. He pulled me in after a tutorial and gave me the "old Richard, my boy" speech. He thought I started the rumor. Me. Shit. "Richard, my boy, it's said you're doing unenviable things to my wife. My boy, that particular assignment has already been well seen to. It's not like you to claim credit for someone else's work." You ever tried to do a paper for someone who thinks you've been saying you're screwing his wife? Shit. Poor old fairy. Boy, what a fucking mess.

(BOB *comes in the front door.*)

RUTH. Hey, Bob, you got your grades.

BOB. Oh, yeah? (*He looks.*)

RUTH. How'd you do?

BOB. Okay. This for Kathy?

RUTH. Yeah. (BOB *starts to open* KATHY'**s** *letter.*) Hey, that's private property.

BOB. What the fuck's gotten into you all of a sudden? (*Reads.*) A, A, A, A . . . B minus. B minus in Poetry 210. B minus. Man, she really went to pieces, without us. I hope she hasn't had a nervous breakdown or anything. Whew, B minus.

(*A knock on the door.* DICK *opens it. It's* LUCKY.)

LUCKY. Listen: I just seen Mr. Willis. He wants you out by tomorrow night.

BOB. How ya been, Lucky?

LUCKY. What? Oh, yeah. Well, if you want a hand, you know where to find me.

RUTH. Thanks a lot, buddy.

LUCKY. Don't get fresh, girlie, don't give me lip. You can talk how you want when you're with your own kind, but you show some respect when you're with Lucky. Smart alecks. Think you know everything. You don't, you don't know . . . you don't know what it's like living living downstairs. That's something I know about. I know about living downstairs. I live downstairs. You seen me . . . you seen me out there, sitting out there. Well, you seen me . . .

BOB. Yeah, yeah, lots of times.

LUCKY. All right. That's what I mean. I sit out there. I'm out there. I got my Budweiser. I got my pretzels. Oh yeah . . . I'm not just sitting out there, you know. I'm watching. I'm keeping my eyes open. (*He's slowly going into a trance.*) I see them cars go by, all them cars. Fords. I see Fords out there. Chevies. Lincolns. Oldsmobiles. Plymouths. I see the odd Cadillac, oh yeah, don't worry about that. It's all up here. You think I'm just sitting there with my Budweiser and pretzels. Think you know it all, oh yeah.

DICK. Don't worry, we took care of it.

LUCKY. Huh?

DICK. We did like you said. Got rid of those plastic garbage cans and got some galvanized aluminum.

LUCKY. All right, that's what I mean. Now, if you want any help, I'll tell you what wou do. You come downstairs. Okay? (*As* LUCKY *goes, we see him look around and call* "Kitty-Kitty.")

RUTH. Guess I'll pack. (*Gets up to leave.* DICK *starts taking down one of his posters.*)

BOB. Where's everyone?

RUTH. Mike and Mel went out with Norman. They're meeting Shelly at the flicks. *Casablanca*. You should see the marks they got. They're both Magna cum.

DICK. Magna cum. Sneaky bastards.

RUTH. Yep. (*She goes out down hall.*)

DICK. You staying for graduation?

BOB. No, you?

DICK. (*Shakes head "no."*) Hey, you really going into the army?

BOB. Yeah, as a hostage. I don't know. What are you doing?

DICK. I don't know.

BOB. Anything lined up for the summer?

DICK. Yeah, delivering milk. It's your friendly college graduate, Mrs. Miller. "Such a shame, the boy went to college." Maybe I'll get sterilized, save any kids having to go through all this. She really was a bitch, you know.

BOB. I guess so.

DICK. Guess so, shit, I hope she gets cancer of the tits and suffers like crazy while she's dying. Honest to Christ, she's the first person I ever met I could really kill.

BOB. Yeah.

DICK. Oh, great humility scene.

BOB. No, it's just, you know, that's how it goes.

DICK. You know something, Bob? You know what's wrong with you?

BOB. I been waiting all this time for someone to tell me. What's wrong with me, Dick?

DICK. You let her get your balls, Bob.

BOB. That was pretty careless, wasn't it?

DICK. No shit, Bob. I remember when you got stung by that bee in the Humanities quadrangle. I always wondered about that. I mean you're supposed to yell when something like that happens. You don't stand there wondering if you should say something. You're really dead, you know.

BOB. Yeah, well, that's what I was trying to tell everyone right before Christmas, I thought I might just try it out, you know, being dead. Didn't feel any different.

DICK. I don't get it.

BOB. No, it's a pretty weird thing. (*Pause.*)

DICK. I gotta pack.
BOB. Yeah.

(DICK *leaves the room.* MIKE *and* COOTIE *burst in through the front door, panting heavily.*)

MIKE. Oh shit, man, we've really had it. Christ, how could the guy do it? I thought he was kidding.

(RUTH *comes in with a small suitcase.*)

RUTH. Hey, you guys better hurry up and pack. We gotta be out of here tomorrow.
COOTIE. Ruth, sit down, huh? Something pretty bad just happened. Seriously, no shitting around.
RUTH. Where's Norman?
COOTIE. Norman's . . . he just . . . oh shit.
MIKE. He set himself on fire.
BOB. He what?
MIKE. All that stuff he was reading. He just . . . I don't know. He got this idea. Oh, fuck, how could the stupid bastard ever . . . ? Shit.
RUTH. I thought you guys were going to see *Casablanca.*
MIKE. No, we had to tell you that. He had this plan. Honest to shit, we didn't know he was serious. Him and Shelly. We thought he's just . . . we went on to the common and he just took all his clothes off and poured gasoline all over him.
COOTIE. We were just shitting around, Ruth. Honest. If we thought he was serious we'd've stopped him, you know.
MIKE. It was that fucking Shelly
RUTH. You fucking, stupid . . .
MIKE. I'm telling you, it wasn't our fault. He wouldn't have lit the match. I know he poured the gasoline, but he'd never've lit the match.
BOB. He's . . .

MIKE. Oh shit, it was awful. He just sat there turning black. I didn't want to look, but I couldn't turn away. His skin just, Christ, it just, fell away from his face and his blood. (*Puts head in hand.*)

RUTH. Stupid, fucking guys. You should've known. Where's Shelly?

COOTIE. She went crazy, Ruth. She just cracked up. She's okay now. We had to practically knock her out. She's coming.

(SHELLY *comes in the front door. Her eyes are closed and her fists clenched.* RUTH *runs to her, doesn't know to do.*)

RUTH. Shelly. Oh, Shelly, Jesus . . .
SHELLY. (*Teeth clenched.*) Fucking guys.

(NORMAN *comes in. He's soaking wet and carries a gasoline can.* MIKE *and* COOTIE *rise.*)

MIKE. See, everything cool now. Everybody trusts each other. That's what it's all about. (*Smiles oddly at the others.*)

COOTIE. (*Registering it all.*) Holy shit! Hey, Mike! (MIKE *and* COOTIE *leave the room.*)

SHELLY. (*Yells.*) Creeps. (*To* RUTH.) You got any first-aid stuff?

RUTH. Yeah. (*Gets a box from the pantry. It's a huge white box with a red cross on it, obviously stolen.*)

BOB. Hey, what happened?

NORMAN. (*Sits.*) I'm all right.

SHELLY. Don't talk, Norman. Would you make him some coffee?

RUTH. Yeah. Those guys said you burned yourself.

NORMAN. No, I'm okay.

(RUTH *makes coffee while* SHELLY *ties a bandage around* NORMAN'S *wrist.*)

SHELLY. Sorry if this hurts. Hey, Ruth, those guys are really bastards. They gotta learn you don't joke around sometimes.

BOB. Hey, were you really gonna burn yourself?

NORMAN. Well, you know . . .

SHELLY. We were all supposed to do it. All four of us. We waited all this time for them to graduate with good grades and everything. Six months almost. I mean, like, the war could've ended. Fucking creeps. They went and put water in the gasoline can.

NORMAN. I think I might be getting a cold.

SHELLY. We're making coffee, Norman. Keep cool.

BOB. Hey, were you really serious?

NORMAN. Well, I thought, you know, with the war and everything . . .

SHELLY. Water, shit.

NORMAN. Well, there was some gas in that can.

SHELLY. Fucking creeps.

NORMAN. I definitely smelled some gas when I poured it over me.

SHELLY. Hold still, Norman.

NORMAN. I mean, I knew there was something wrong when I kept holding the match to my wrist and nothing happened.

SHELLY. What do you mean, nothing happened? What's wrong with you, Norman? You call that burn on your wrist nothing? It's the worst burn I ever saw. We're lucky we didn't get arrested.

NORMAN. I've seen movies of the Buddhist monks setting themselves on fire. They usually go up pretty quick in the movies. I bet it hurts a lot. My wrist really hurts.

RUTH. (*Brings* NORMAN *some coffee.*) Listen, we have to be out of here by tomorrow.

NORMAN. All right.

RUTH. Well, what are you gonna do?

NORMAN. I haven't thought about it. I thought I was going to be dead by now. I hadn't planned beyond that.

RUTH. You got a place to stay?

SHELLY. He'll stay with me.

NORMAN. Yeah, okay.

RUTH. We'll have to have a big clean-up in case Willis comes around.

NORMAN. I was thinking maybe I'll try to get back into graduate school. I'm sick of washing dishes.

BOB. (*Has been taking down his map of Europe from the wall.*) I think I'll go to Europe.

NORMAN. I'm not really angry at Mel and Mike. In a way I'm kind of glad I'm not dead.

SHELLY. I think those two guys are really evil.

(RUTH *goes down the hall.*)

BOB. You ever been to France?

SHELLY. I went last summer.

BOB. What's it like?

SHELLY. Shitty. They're really uptight in France. I got busted in Calais. Two weeks in prison with the runs. That's no joke.

BOB. Maybe England.

NORMAN. I was in England once.

BOB. What's it like?

NORMAN. I guess it was a pretty valuable experience. I remember thinking at the time my horizons were a lot wider after that trip. Maybe I'll go back there one day.

BOB. Oh well, there's always Italy or Greece.

SHELLY. If you go over there, check out Algeria. Algeria's really something else.

WILLIS. (*Opens the door.*) Okay if I step in? Hey, what have you done to your arm?

NORMAN. It's just a burn.

WILLIS. Too bad, huh? Look, how's about if I see everyone for a minute? Everybody here?

BOB. (*Yelling.*) DICK, RUTH, MIKE, COOTIE, C'MERE A MINUTE. MR. WILLIS WANTS US.

WILLIS. Hey, hey, hey, you don't have to do that. You don't have to yell on account of me. (*All come in.*)

Hi, how's everybody? Gettin' ready for the big day? You gonna wear them long robes and everything, hey? All that fancy ceremony. Pretty good, huh? Listen, I just wanna give the place a quick once-over because I'll tell you why. I got this tenant moving in pretty soon so I gotta be sure everything's okay. Get rid of them milk bottles, that's the first thing, and I'll pick up the rent for this month, okay? How 'bout this floor, huh? You gonna finish it? Hey, I asked a question, who's supposed to be doing this floor?

BOB. I am, Mr. Willis.

WILLIS. So how come you leave it half finished?

BOB. Sorry, I never got the time.

WILLIS. Well, you get it. I give you good money for them tiles, put me back a hunnerd bucks. How many landlords you find'll do that?

BOB. Yeah, okay.

WILLIS. By tomorrow night, understand. Now, let's have a little look round. (WILLIS *goes down the hall followed by* BOB, RUTH, COOTIE *and* MIKE *and* DICK.)

NORMAN. Mike. (MIKE *turns.*) Listen, I just want to tell you, I'm not angry about what happened.

MIKE. What do you mean?

SHELLY. You're a real creep pulling a trick like that.

MIKE. That's what I get for saving his life?

SHELLY. It's none of your business. It's the existential right of every living person to take his own life.

MIKE. No one's stopping you now.

NORMAN. What I wanted to say is if you and Mel are coming back next year to go to graduate school, maybe we can share a place. I mean, you know, I could come down here early and look around.

MIKE. You going home for the summer?

SHELLY. He's staying with me.

NORMAN. Yeah, well, I might go home for a few weeks. Visit my folks. The best way is you write to my father, care of the Police Department, Erie County, and if I'm not at home he'll know where to forward it.

MIKE. Police Department, Erie County.

NORMAN. Yeah, or you can put Commissioner of Police, Erie County. It'll reach him either way. Just put, "Forward to Norman."

MIKE. Right. Me and Cootie'll be up in the great Northwest Territory helping Dad with the furs. If you don't hear from us just go ahead and find a place for all of us 'cause sometimes the mail gets delayed.

NORMAN. Don't worry, I'll get a place.

MIKE. Commissioner of Police, Erie County, New York.

NORMAN. That's right. (MIKE *smiles at him, not without warmth. In come* COOTIE, RUTH, BOB, DICK *and* MR. WILLIS.)

WILLIS. Not bad. I'll tellya what I'll do. I'll keep the fifty-dollar deposit for holes in the plaster and the broken window.

COOTIE. Hey, we didn't break that window. That was broken when we moved in.

WILLIS. That's not my problem, Cootie. I keep the fifty and if any of you guys got an objection you want to take it up with me let's have it. Look, I got a living to make like everybody else in town. Maybe you think I'm being a rotten guy, but you wait. You go out there in the world and you're gonna see things you'll think old Willis was Snow White . . . and the seven dwarfs all rolled into one. You're gonna see dishonesty, you're gonna see mean people. You see swindlers, killers, crooks, you see, you know, that hamburger they got on sale now; 90 percent fat. Ninety percent. I don't know. There was a time I can remember you paid your taxes you knew your money was going into the right things, good, wholesome things. Look at it now'days. Two blocks away there's a house full of guys known all over the neighborhood to practice open homosexuality. Open homosexuality two blocks away and there's kids playing outside that house every day. I'll tell you, you gotta save this poor fuckin' country. Excuse my language, but it's true. (*Pause.*) I'm gonna miss having you kids around. I know it sounds kinda corny. God bless you kids and good luck. I'll take a check for the rent.

COOTIE. (*Sings: Others joining in.*)
> For he's a jolly good fellow,
> For he's a jolly good fellow,
> For he's a jolly good fellow,
> That nobody can deny.
> That nobody can deny.
> That nobody can deny.
> (*Etc. all the way through.*)

(*At first* WILLIS *beams, but during the song they all start laughing at him, and as they laugh they leave the room, still singing sloppily.* WILLIS *is left behind with* SHELLY, *who is crying. Fade.*)

END SCENE TWO

ACT TWO

SCENE 3

The next afternoon. The kitchen is bare of furniture. Ice-box is gone, only a few milk bottles left. Only one chair left. BOB *is laying the vinyl tiles.*

COOTIE *comes into the room with his* FATHER. *He grabs the last valise by the front door.*

COOTIE. Hey, Bob, I'm going.
BOB. Yeah, we'll see you.
COOTIE. Yeah.

(MIKE *comes into the kitchen from the hall door.*)

MIKE. You going?

COOTIE. Yeah. Oh, this is my father. That's Mike, that's Bob.

BOB. Hi.

MIKE. Hi.

FATHER. A pleasure.

MIKE. What?

FATHER. It's a pleasure meeting you.

MIKE. Oh yeah, right.

COOTIE. Well, see you guys. Hey, what you doing next year?

BOB. Oh, I got a job in a department store.

COOTIE. Playing piano?

BOB. Harp.

COOTIE. Great. Well, see ya.

BOB. See ya.

MIKE. Yeah, see ya, Cootie.

COOTIE. Yeah.

FATHER. Nice meeting you boys.

COOTIE. Ah, Dad? (*Leaves with his* FATHER.)

MIKE. They don't look like each other. Good old Cootie. Where's Norman?

BOB. He left about an hour ago.

MIKE. Never said good-bye or anything.

BOB. You should've seen it, putting all his stuff in the back of a police car.

MIKE. What?

BOB. Yeah, his old man's Commissioner of Police, or something.

MIKE. I'll be fucked.

(RUTH *comes in from the hall with two suitcases and sets them down by some other suitcases near the door.*)

RUTH. I guess that's it. Where's Cootie?

MIKE. He just left with his dad.

RUTH. Some friend. No good-bye or anything.

MIKE. We'll see him next year.

RUTH. No, we won't.

(MIKE *and* RUTH *go down the hall for their last luggage.* DICK *and the* MILKMAN *enter through the front door with empty cartons. They load the remaining bottles.*)

DICK. Hey, I wouldn't mind a little help, here. I gotta catch a train.

MILKMAN. I don't understand you guys. You're supposed to be college graduates. Eight hundred and fifty-seven two-quart milk bottles. That's not the kind of thing a grown-up person does. You're supposed to be grownups. I don't get it.

(*The PHONE IS RINGING.*)

DICK. That's the last one.

MILKMAN. Okay. I just hope you guys don't think you can go through life hoarding milk bottles like this. I got enough to do without this. I got a regular route. (*To* DICK.) Look, if you want to pick up a lot of bottles, put your finger right down inside, you get more that way.

DICK. Okay. Hey, you guys, you're a lot of help.

(MILKMAN *and* DICK *go out with their cartons.*)

BOB. (*Answering phone.*) Hello, oh yes, how are you? No, this is Bob. Bob Rettie. No, music. Yes, of course I remember you. No, he's not in right now.

(MIKE *and* RUTH *re-enter and motion* BOB *that they have to go. He motions back that it's okay. He waves good-bye as they pick up their suitcases and leave.*)

RUTH. Hey, good luck.
BOB. Yeah, yeah, you too. See ya, Mike.

MIKE. See ya. (RUTH *and* MIKE *exit.*)

BOB. (*Back on the phone.*) Sorry, Mrs. Roper, I was just saying good-bye to some people I . . . (*Quiet irony.*) . . . some friends of mine. (*Pause.*) I don't think he'll be back but I can leave a message, you know, in case . . . (*Pause.*) Look, Mrs. Roper, I'm sorry about that but there's nothing I can do if he's gone. Hey, calm down . . . look, I think I'd better hang up now, O.K.? Listen, I'm gonna hang up. Good-bye. (*Hangs up quickly as* DICK *breezes in through the front door.*)

DICK. Boy, that guy was sure pissed off about the milk bottles. You should've seen the look on his face.

BOB. Hey, you know that guy you studied with? Professor Roper?

DICK. (*Stopping. Cautious.*) Yeah.

BOB. His wife just called.

DICK. What'd she want?

BOB. She just . . . I don't know. Nothing, I guess. Pretty weird.

DICK. Yeah. Pretty weird. (*Takes up his bag and heads for the front door. He confronts* KATHY, *who is just entering.*)

KATHY. Hi. Can I come in? (DICK *moves aside. He and* BOB *stare at* KATHY. *This makes her a little nervous.*) Everyone gone?

DICK. }
BOB. }   (*Together.*) Yeah. . . .

(*They exchange a nervous glance.*)

BOB. Except for me and Dick. We're still here. We're right in front of you, as a matter of fact . . .

DICK. That's a nice coat she's wearing. That's a very nice coat, Kathy.

KATHY. (*Knows something is going on but doesn't know what.*) Thanks.

BOB. Hey, Dick. (DICK *leaves.*) See ya. (*To himself.*)

KATHY. Finishing the floor?

BOB. Evidently.

KATHY. Kind of late, isn't it? (*Pause.*) Did they send my grades here?

BOB. Right there. You did really shitty.

KATHY. (*Gets the letter.*) Bob, listen . . . I'm sorry about . . . sounds pretty silly.

BOB. No, I accept your apology for whatever you think you did.

KATHY. I saw Ruth the other day. She said you've been . . . well, pretty bad this semester.

BOB. Did she say that?

KATHY. I wish I'd known . . . couldn't you have . . . you should have told me to stay.

BOB. Well, it slipped my mind. Sorry.

KATHY. You shouldn't be so ashamed of your feelings.

BOB. Okay.

KATHY. I'm serious. You've gotta learn to let go. Like with your music. It's all squenched and tidy.

BOB. Okay. I'll work on that.

KATHY. Oh, Bob.

BOB. What?

KATHY. I really wish you'd've told me. I'd've come back. I never really related to Richard.

BOB. I'll tell him when I see him.

KATHY. Yeah, you're right. Why the hell should you be nice? Oh well, good luck . . . and, you know, when you see your mother say hello for me.

BOB. Okay.

KATHY. How is she?

BOB. She's okay. Sort of dead.

KATHY. I like her, Bob. You're lucky. She's, you know, she's a real person.

BOB. No, she's you know, a real corpse.

KATHY. All right, have it your way.

BOB. No, it's not what I wanted particularly. No, taken all in all, from various different angles, I'd've preferred it if she lived. I'm pretty sure of that.

KATHY. (*Pause:*) She's not really.

BOB. School's over.

KATHY. Bob, do you know what you're saying?

BOB. Kathy, please get the fuck out of here.

KATHY. But, I mean, Ruth never told me . . . Didn't you tell anyone?

BOB. Yeah, I just told you.

KATHY. But, I mean . . . when . . . when did . . .

BOB. Christmas. No, no, it was the day after.

KATHY. (*Sits.*) Jesus, Bob, why didn't you tell anyone? I mean, how could you live for six months without telling someone?

BOB. (*No emotion.*) Oh, I don't know. A little cunning. A little fortitude. A little perseverance. (*Pause.*) I couldn't believe it. Not the last time anyway. They put her in this room. I don't know what you call it. They bring everybody there just before they kick the bucket. They just sort of lie there looking at each other, wondering what the hell they got in common to talk about. I couldn't believe that anyone could look like she looked and still be alive. (*Pause.*) She knew. I'm sure of that. (*Pause.*) Once, I remember, she tried to tell me something. I mean this noise came out of somewhere around her mouth, like somebody running a stick over a fence or something, and I thought maybe she's trying to tell me something. So I leaned over to hear better and I caught a whiff of that breath. Like fried puke. And I was sick all over her. (*Pause. Brighter.*) But you want to know something funny, and I mean this really is funny, so you can laugh if you like. There was this lady dying next to my mother and she kept talking about her daughter Susan. Well, Susan came to visit the day I puked on Mom. And you know what? It was only Susan Weinfeld which doesn't mean anything to you but she happens to have been the girl I spent a good many of my best months as a sophomore in high school trying to lay. In fact, her virginity almost cost me a B+ in history and here we were, six years later, staring at each other across two dying mothers. I want to tell you something, Kathy.

She looked fantastic. And I could tell she was thinking
the same thing about me. I mean that kind of scene
doesn't happen every day. It was like . . . (*Thinks.*)
. . . it was like how we were the first time. Maybe, just
possibly, a little better. So we went out and had a coffee
in Mr. Doughnut and started groping each other like
crazy under the counter and I mean we just couldn't keep
our hands off each other so I suggested we get a cab
down to my mother's place since, you know, there happened to be no one there at the moment. But the funniest
thing was when we get down to Mom's place and you
know all those stairs you have to go up and there's Susan
all over me practically screaming for it and I start
fumbling around with the keys in the lock and none of
them would fit. I must've tried every key about fifty
fucking times and none of them would fit. Boy, what a
drag. (*Pause.*) Oh, we got in all right. Finally. I had to
go downstairs, through the Salvatore's apartment, out the
window, up the fire escape and through Mom's place but
when I opened the front door, guess what? There's poor
old Susan asleep on the landing. She really looked cute.
I hated to wake her up. Anyway, by the time we'd made
coffee and talked and smoked about a million cigarettes
each we didn't feel like it any more. Not really. We did
it anyway but, you know, just to be polite, just to make
some sense out of the evening. It was, taken all in all, a
pretty ordinary fuck. The next morning we made plans to
meet again that night. We even joked about it, you
know, about what a super-fucking good time we'd have,
and if you ask me, we could've probably really gotten into
something incredible if we'd tried again, but when I went
to the hospital I found out good old Mom had croaked
sometime during the night and somehow, I still don't
know why to this day . . . I never got in touch with
Susan again. And vice versa. It's a funny thing, you
know. At the funeral there were all these people. Friends
of Mom's— I didn't know any of them. They were all
crying like crazy and I . . . well . . . (*Pause.*) I never

even got to the burial. The car I was in broke down on the Merritt Parkway. Just as well. I didn't feel like seeing all those people. I'd sure love to have fucked Susan again, though.

KATHY. Bob . . . I . . .

BOB. (*Abstract.*) Anyway . . . I just didn't feel like telling anyone. I mean, I wasn't all that upset. I was a little upset, mostly because I thought I ought to be more upset, but as for your actual grief, well. Anything interesting happen to you this semester . . . Kathy? (KATHY *has risen.*) Going? (KATHY *is going out the door.*) Give my regards to that guy you're rescuing at the moment, what's-his-name. (KATHY *is gone.* BOB *shrugs. The cat wanders in from the hallway.*) Hey, cat, what are you doing hanging around here? All the humans gone west. (*Puts the cat outside and shuts the door. He nudges the tiles with his toe and looks around at the empty room.*) Hey, guys, guess what happened to me. I want to tell you about this really incredible thing that happened to me . . . (*He is faltering now, choking slightly but he doesn't know he's about to crack. His body is doing something strange, unfamiliar.*) Hey, what's happening . . . (*He's crying now.*) Oh fuck, come on, come on. Shit, no, no . . .

FADE

END OF PLAY

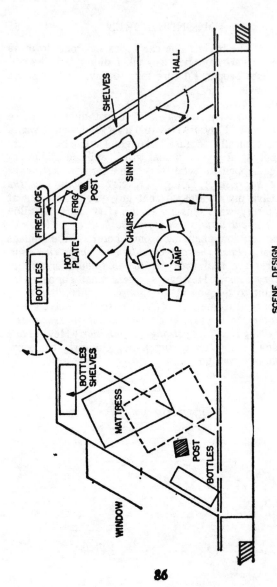

SCENE DESIGN
"MOONCHILDREN"

86

Other Publications for Your Interest

HUSBANDRY
(LITTLE THEATRE—DRAMA)

By PATRICK TOVATT

2 men, 2 women—Interior

At its recent world premiere at the famed Actors Theatre of Louisville, this enticing new drama moved an audience of theatre professionals up off their seats and on to their feet to cheer. Mr. Tovatt has given us an insightful drama about what is happening to the small, family farm in America—and what this means for the future of the country. The scene is a farmhouse whose owners are on the verge of losing their farm. They are visited by their son and his wife, who live "only" eight hours' drive away. The son has a good job in the city, and his wife does, too. The son, Harry, is really put on the horns of a dilemma when he realizes that he is his folks' only hope. The old man can't go it alone anymore—and he needs his son. Pulling at him from the other side is his wife, who does not want to leave her job and uproot her family to become a farm wife. *Husbandry*, then, is ultimately about what it means to be a *husband*—both in the farm and in the family sense. *Variety* praised the "delicacy of Tovatt's dialogue", and called the play "a literate exploration of family responsibilities in a mobile society." Said *Time*: "The play simmers so gently for so long, as each potential confrontation is deflected with Chekhovian shrugs and silences, that when it boils into hostility it sears the audience."   (#10169)

CLARA'S PLAY
(LITTLE THEATRE—DRAMA)

By JOHN OLIVE

3 men, 1 woman—Exterior

Clara, an aging spinster, lives alone in a remote farmhouse. She is the last surviving member of one of the area's most prominent families. It is summer, 1915. Enter an immigrant, feisty soul named Sverre looking for a few days' work before moving on. But Clara's farm needs more than just a few days' work, and Sverre stays on to help Clara fix up and run the farm. It soon becomes clear unscrupulous local businessmen are bilking Clara out of money and hope to gain control of her property. Sverre agrees to stay on to help Clara keep her family's property. "A story of determination, loyalty. It has more than a measure of love, of resignation, of humor and loyalty."—Chicago Sun-Times. "A playwright of unusual sensitivity in delineating character and exploring human relationships." —Chicago Tribune. "Gracefully-written, with a real sense of place."—Village Voice. A recent success both at Chicago's fine Wisdom Bridge Theatre and at the Great American Play Festival of the world-reknowned Actors Theatre of Louisville; and, on tour, starring Jean Stapleton.   (#5076)

Other Publications for Your Interest

A WEEKEND NEAR MADISON
(LITTLE THEATRE—COMIC DRAMA)
By KATHLEEN TOLAN

2 men, 3 women—Interior

This recent hit from the famed Actors Theatre of Louisville, a terrific ensemble play about male-female relationships in the 80's, was praised by *Newsweek* as "warm, vital, glowing . . . full of wise ironies and unsentimental hopes". The story concerns a weekend reunion of old college friends now in their early thirties. The occasion is the visit of Vanessa, the queen bee of the group, who is now the leader of a lesbian/feminist rock band. Vanessa arrives at the home of an old friend who is now a psychiatrist hand in hand with her naif-like lover, who also plays in the band. Also on hand are the psychiatrist's wife, a novelist suffering from writer's block; and his brother, who was once Vanessa's lover and who still loves her. In the course of the weekend, Vanessa reveals that she and her lover desperately want to have a child—and she tries to persuade her former male lover to father it, not understanding that he might have some feelings about the whole thing. *Time Magazine* heard "the unmistakable cry of an infant hit . . . Playwright Tolan's work radiates promise and achievement." (#25051)

PASTORALE
(LITTLE THEATRE—COMEDY)
By DEBORAH EISENBERG

3 men, 4 women—Interior
(plus 1 or 2 bit parts and 3 optional extras)

"Deborah Eisenberg is one of the freshest and funniest voices in some seasons."—Newsweek. Somewhere out in the country Melanie has rented a house and in the living room she, her friend Rachel who came for a weekend but forgets to leave, and their school friend Steve (all in their mid-20s) spend nearly a year meandering through a mental landscape including such concerns as phobias, friendship, work, sex, slovenliness and epistemology. Other people happen by: Steve's young girlfriend Celia, the virtuous and annoying Edie, a man who Melanie has picked up in a bar, and a couple who appear during an intense conversation and observe the sofa is on fire. The lives of the three friends inevitably proceed and eventually draw them, the better prepared perhaps by their months on the sofa, in separate directions. "The most original, funniest new comic voice to be heard in New York theater since Beth Henley's 'Crimes of the Heart.'"—N.Y. Times. "A very funny, stylish comedy."—The New Yorker. "Wacky charm and wayward wit."—New York Magazine. "Delightful."—N.Y. Post. "Uproarious . . . the play is a world unto itself, and it spins."—N.Y. Sunday Times. (#18016)